ALPINE PLANTS
Ecology for Gardeners

ALPINE PLANTS
Ecology for Gardeners

John E G Good and David Millward

In nature there are neither
rewards nor punishments;
there are consequences

Robert G Ingersoll (1833-1899)

BATSFORD

First published in the United Kingdom in 2007 by
Batsford
151 Freston Road
London
W10 6TH

An imprint of Anova Books Company Ltd.

ISBN 0 7134 9017 9
ISBN (13-digit) 9780713490176

A CIP catalogue record for this book is available from the British Library.

10 9 8 7 6 5 4 3 2 1

Reproduction by Anorax Imaging Ltd., Leeds
Printed and bound by Craft Print International Ltd., Singapore

This book can be ordered direct from the publisher at the website: www.anovabooks.com
or from the Alpine Garden Society at the website: www.alpinegardensociety.net
Or try your local bookshop

CONTENTS

ACKNOWLEDGEMENTS

This book could not have been written without the help and enthusiasm of many people. First and foremost I would like to thank Dr David Millward, who plugged one of the principal gaps in my knowledge of alpine plant ecology when he offered to write the chapter on geology and soils. I could not have wished for a better person, since David is one of that rare breed, a professional geologist with a keen interest in alpine gardening. Many other people have helped me in all sorts of ways. Fellow ecologists have helped, through what they have written on alpine ecology and through the many discussions I have had with them; I have drawn heavily on the published research of Professor Christian Körner of the University of Basel (Switzerland), which he drew together in his seminal book, *Alpine Plant Life – Functional Plant Ecology of High Mountain Systems*, published in 1999. Professor John Birks, Dr William Bowman, Professor Terry Callaghan, Professor Richard Crawford, Professor Norman Deno, Dr Noranne Ellis, Professor Chris Gliddon, Professor Mark Hill, Dr Barbara Jones, Dr Halina Piekos-Mirkowa, Professor David Rankin, Professor John Richards and the late Professor Alan Smith are other professional scientists who have particularly influenced my thinking. Of equal value, especially in helping me to provide some (albeit limited) advice on the practical application of knowledge of the ecology of alpines in the wild to their cultivation in gardens, have been the many discussions with fellow enthusiasts in the Alpine Garden Society, the Scottish Rock Garden Club and the North American Rock Garden Society. It seems invidious to mention individuals when I have discussed these matters with so many people, but I must particularly thank Ron Beeston, Pete Boardman, Brian Burrow, Peter Cunnington, Jack Elliott, Peter Erskine, Alan Furness, Jane McGary, Drs Keith and Rachel Lever, David Mowle, Dr John Page, Robert Rolfe, Gerald Taaffe, Frank Tindall, and a number of friends who are sadly no longer with us: Lionel Bacon, Roy Elliott, Eric Hilton, Duncan Lowe, Wayne Roderick, Dr George Smith and Dr Don Stead. The journals of the AGS and kindred societies have also provided me with a rich source of information, as have various internet sites, in recent years, notably Alpine-L, which I recommend to all enthusiasts. Those who have kindly lent me photographs for use in this book are acknowledged in the list of colour plates. Of these, Kit Grey-Wilson and Robert Rolfe deserve special mention for their kindness in spending time reading through my manuscript and making useful suggestions for its improvement.

Finally, my heartfelt thanks go to my wife Pam, who has accompanied me on many of my trips to the mountains, and without whose tolerance and good humour I would probably not have finished this book. I therefore dedicate it to her.

John Good, January 24, 2006

LIST OF PLATES, WITH PHOTO CREDITS

JEGG – John Good   AGS – Alpine Garden Society   Plant Images – C. Grey-Wilson

Chapter 1
1.1 Plant Images
1.2 JEGG
1.3 JEGG
1.4 JEGG
1.5 JEGG
1.6 Plant Images
1.7 Robert Rolfe
1.8 Plant Images
1.9 JEGG
1.10 Plant Images
1.11 JEGG
1.12 Robert Rolfe
1.13 Plant Images

Chapter 2
2.1 JEGG
2.2 JEGG
2.3 JEGG
2.4 JEGG
2.5 JEGG
2.6 JEGG
2.7 JEGG
2.8 JEGG
2.9 JEGG
2.10 JEGG
2.11 D Millward
2.12 JEGG
2.13 D Millward
2.14 D Millward
2.15 D Millward

Chapter 3
3.1 Robert Rolfe
3.2 JEGG
3.3 Plant Images
3.4 Robert Rolfe
3.5 D Millward
3.6 Plant Images
3.7 JEGG
3.8 JEGG
3.9 Robert Rolfe
3.10 Robert Rolfe
3.11 Robert Rolfe
3.12 JEGG

Chapter 4
4.1 Morag McGrath
4.2 Morag McGrath
4.3 Robert Rolfe
4.4 Robert Rolfe
4.5 Pete Boardman
4.6 AGS Slide Library
4.7 AGS Slide Library
4.8 AGS Slide Library
4.9 Plant Images
4.10 P J Erskine
4.11 JEGG
4.12 Robert Rolfe

Chapter 5
5.1 JEGG
5.2 Plant Images
5.3 AGS Slide Library, Peter Sheasby
5.4 JEGG
5.5 JEGG
5.6 JEGG
5.7 JEGG

Chapter 6
6.1 D Millward
6.2 J Skidmore
6.3 D Millward
6.4 D Millward
6.5 D Millward
6.6 D Millward
6.7 D Millward

Chapter 7
7.1 JEGG
7.2 JEGG
7.3 Plant Images
7.4 JEGG
7.5 D Rankin
7.6 AGS Slide Library
7.7 JEGG

Chapter 8
8.1 JEGG
8.2 JEGG
8.3 JEGG
8.4 Robert Rolfe
8.5 AGS Slide Library, Peter Sheasby
8.6 JEGG
8.7 JEGG
8.8 JEGG
8.9 P J Erskine
8.10 JEGG
8.11 JEGG
8.12 JEGG

Chapter 9
9.1 JEGG
9.2 JEGG
9.3 JEGG
9.4 P J Erskine
9.4 AGS Slide Library

Chapter 10
10.1 JEGG
10.2 JEGG
10.3 AGS Slide Library, Peter Sheasby
10.4 AGS Slide Library, Peter Sheasby

PREFACE

The cold desert tundras and windswept wastes that are found above the tree line on mountains, and beyond the tree line in sub-polar regions, are among the most hostile environments on earth. The plant species that live in these extreme conditions do so as the result of a long-evolved ability to survive in places too hostile for less well adapted species. Their number is greater than might be expected: about 3 per cent of the world's land surface lies above or beyond the timber line but approximately 6 per cent of the world's flowering plants (c. 12,000 species, in 2,000 genera and 100 families) occur there. The aim of this book is to investigate the challenges that these many and varied plants must overcome to survive in sub-polar and alpine environments, as well as the solutions they have evolved to overcome them. Also, to indicate how this knowledge can help us to cultivate them better.

My justifications for writing the book are threefold. The first is that, to the best of my knowledge, no book exists that attempts to interpret what we know in detail of the ecology of alpine plants for the benefit of the keen alpine gardener. The second is that the substantial body of information available on the ecology of alpine plants is scattered widely in specialist books, scientific papers and in the field notes of botanists and plant collectors – and as such it is unavailable to most alpine gardeners. The third is that, having given many talks on this subject to groups of alpine gardeners at home and abroad, I have received frequent requests that the information be made available in book form.

One aspect of this book that may irritate some readers springs from the fact that ecologists choose species for study because of their intrinsic scientific interest, rather than their aesthetic appeal or potential horticultural usefulness. Thus while many references to familiar garden alpines will appear, plant names that are much less familiar or unknown to most alpine gardeners will also crop up. But, even though we may never wish to grow these plants in our gardens, understanding how they tick may help us in growing their more garden-worthy brethren.

1·INTRODUCTION

The word 'ecology' is derived from the Greek *oikos*, meaning house, or household. Thus, the science of ecology is the study of the relationship between organisms and their environment. Most people reading this book will be gardeners who grow alpine plants. By improving their understanding of the ecology of alpines, they hope to grow the plants better in their gardens. By the time they reach the end of this book, some readers may also find the subject of such intrinsic interest that they will be encouraged to seek out further information from the references provided in the bibliography or – even better – by making their own observations in the mountains. The latter are to be recommended, since there are many grey areas in alpine ecology where understanding is still minimal; I will draw attention to some of these at various points.

The systems within which ecological relationships operate include non-living as well as living components and are known as ecosystems. Thus there are grassland ecosystems, forest ecosystems, lake ecosystems and many others, as well as the arctic-alpine ecosystems that are the chief focus of this book. The ecosystem is a useful concept in ecology, providing a comparative framework for the definition and description of particular plant and animal communities, and their environmental characteristics. It allows us to say what is special about particular communities, and consequently to understand what needs to be special about the plants and animals from which they are formed. Chapter 2 provides more information about ecosystems in general and alpine ecosystems in particular.

Because of their proximity to European centres of botanical and horticultural learning, the Alps were the setting for most early ecological observations on mountain plants. Early attempts at cultivation were correspondingly aimed at mimicking alpine conditions. Things have moved on, and today ecologists study – and gardeners grow – plants from all the mountain ranges of the world. But the collective noun 'alpines' is too well established in everyday horticultural parlance to be changed, so we are forever 'alpine gardeners' – even if we grow only plants from the Antipodes or the Americas. There is no harm in this misnomer as long as we realize that many mountainous areas actually have very different environments from those found in the Alps; the conditions provided for true Alpines in the garden may be quite unsuitable for plants from other mountain ranges. In addition, we need to be aware that, in many cases, knowledge of the remoter mountain regions of the world, and of the ecology of their plants, is still rudimentary. In attempting to provide suitable growing conditions, we often have to rely on reports of plant hunting trips in the journals of the Alpine Gardening Society or similar publications, or the field notes of botanists and seed collectors. Needless to say, any additional information that can be recorded by travellers in these remote mountain regions is particularly welcome, because it will surely lead to improved success rates when cultivating these plants.

Perhaps I should grasp the nettle early on and define what I mean by an 'alpine' in the context of this book. I am inclined to be pedantic, not because of any inborn hostility to lowland plants being grown among mountain plants (if they look right together, that's fine by me), but because alpine plant ecology is just that – the ecology of alpine plants. In general terms the best definition of alpine plants is 'plants that grow above or beyond the tree line'. In this context, latitude rather than altitude is the chief factor in determining the tree line, and 'beyond' refers to plants growing in sub-Arctic and sub-Antarctic regions. If we can learn how plants from these most extreme alpine (**Plate 1.1**) and sub-polar environments cope in the wild, and can be tamed in cultivation, we are likely to find the remainder from less challenging habitats relatively easy to deal with.

Plant growth rates are generally low in alpine environments, whether temperate or tropical. Slow growth rates would be expected in temperate mountains, given the short growing season and often infertile soils. Dry season drought stress, especially during unusually dry years, appears to be a key factor in some tropical alpine areas. More generally, the large diurnal temperature fluctuations that characterize most tropical mountains impose severe constraints on plant growth. But it is worth noting that the slow growth rates of high alpines persist even in the low-altitude garden, where the plants have much more favourable growing conditions. Compare, for instance, the

Above: 1.1 Extreme alpine environment high above the tree line in the upper Sabche Khola, Nepal.

11

Above: 1.2 *Campanula cenisia* like many high alpines has a very slow growth rate. Italian alps.

Above: 1.4 Mountain goat grazing alpine vegetation. Glacier, Waterton National Park, Montana.

dry weight biomass produced in a single growing season by a Canterbury bell with that of its high alpine cousins *Campanula cenisia* (**Plate 1.2**) or *C. piperi*. The reasons for this persistent slow growth rate are considered in Chapter 3.

One of the most oft-quoted growth characteristics of alpine plants is their high ratio of roots to shoots. Many of us have observed this, marvelling at the extent of the root system produced by the tiny seedlings of high alpine cushion plants. Whereas a typical border perennial plant will produce considerably more shoots than roots in a growing season, the reverse is often the case for alpines (**Plate 1.3**). This contrasting allocation of resources will also be discussed in Chapter 3.

Herbivory appears to have an important, often overlooked, influence on alpine plant productivity and community structure. One might assume that there are few large herbivores grazing in the high mountains, and few invertebrate pests feeding at the individual plant scale. But careful observation reveals that this is generally not the case. Even in mountain areas, where the influence of domestic grazing animals is limited, (which is in relatively few), there are wild beasts such as goats (**Plate 1.4**), marmots and squirrels, often feeding right up to the limits of vegetation. And while invertebrate herbivores (such as slugs, snails, beetles, caterpillars and aphids) may be less diverse and less numerous in the mountains than in the lowlands, they are feeding on plants that are growing relatively slowly, and are consequently more vulnerable. Also, as in the lowlands, there are many specialist root feeders that do their damage out of sight and unnoticed. Pests and diseases of wild and cultivated plants will be discussed more fully in Chapter 3.

Above: 1.3 Demonstration of the large proportion of roots to shoots in the alpine cushion plant (*Androsace carnea*) top, compared with a lowland herb (*Chrysanthemum parthenium*), bottom.

While the Arctic-Alpine zone is always a harsh habitat, it is important to realize that it can be a very variable one. There may be considerable variation within the same mountain range, and even on the same mountain, let alone between mountains in different regions of the world. These differences are due to a range of interacting factors relating to both space and time. Variations in macro- and microclimate are particularly influential. Macroclimate is influenced in turn by factors such as latitude, distance from the sea (continentality), the direction of prevailing winds and their sources (sea or land) and position relative to other mountain ranges (notably the rain shadow effect that produces dry areas on regions to the leeward side of mountains). Microclimatic influences may be less obvious but are nonetheless profound. They may be engendered by such factors as position relative to the midday sun in summer, micro-topography (especially where it influences the depth and duration of snow lie, which is often of critical importance in determining species distributions – see Chapter 5) and the influence of surrounding vegetation. Both the causes and significance of these climatic influences are described in detail in Chapter 4.

Within the alpine zone above the tree line there is marked zonation of vegetation. Although the nature of the plant communities in the different zones varies greatly in relation to climatic and edaphic (soil-related) factors, certain trends are found in most temperate and many tropical mountains. Coarse meadow grasses, tall herbs and erect shrubs often dominate the vegetation near the tree line, sometimes intermingled with a few stunted 'krummholz' coniferous trees that have managed to survive beyond the forest edge. Increasing elevation brings a gradual change towards shorter, more compact vegetation. This is made up of non-tussock grasses, small perennial herbs and prostrate shrubs (**Plate 1.5**). In tropical

Left: 1.5 The dwarf shrub, *Daphne cneorum,* growing in a stony alpine meadow. Cirque de Troumose, Pyrenees.

mountains this intermediate zone is often dominated by giant rosette plants, such as the tree lobelias (**Plate 1.6**), the groundsels of eastern Africa and, in the Andes, the montane bromeliads (*Puya* and *Espeletia*) and lupins.

Higher still, the climate gets more severe and the soil becomes more skeletal (often limited to the flatter areas between rock outcrops or to stabilized scree). Here, tundra plants, which would be unable to compete with the coarser vegetation lower down, can come into their own. Cushion plants are particularly characteristic of this high alpine zone, whether growing in the open (**Plate 1.7**) or on the rocks (**Plate 1.8**). They are found in all mountain ranges, although they are less

Above: 1.7 Cushion paramo forms dense ground cover over large areas at high elevations in the Andes.

Far left: 1.6 Giant lobelias (*Lobelia aberdarica*) dot the upper slopes of Mt Elgon, Kenya.

Left: 1.8 Some cushion plants, such as *Androsace vandellii*, seen here in the Pyrenees, are characteristically found growing in rock crevices.

characteristic of tropical montane floras than those of temperate regions. Their universal occurrence provides a good illustration of the phenomenon of convergent evolution, whereby similar harsh environments exert strong selective pressures to produce plants that look alike, even though they may often come from ancestors that are unrelated and morphologically very distinct. Thus we have eritrichiums (**Plate 1.9**) (Boraginaceae), looking more like androsaces (Primulaceae) than forget-me-nots or borage ; the cushion raoulias or 'vegetable sheep' (*Asteraceae*) of New Zealand (**Plate 1.10**), which would never be taken for the daisies that they are, and in the high Andes, the cushion azorellas (Apiaceae), not easily recognizable as members of the carrot family. But not all high alpines are cushions; other well-adapted species such as *Ranunculus glacialis* (**Plate 1.11**), with its thick fleshy leaves, and the Himalayan saussureas, with their woolly covering, are also perfectly adapted to withstand the worst excesses of the high alpine climate.

Above: 1.11 *Ranunculus glacialis* showing thick fleshy foliage. Col de L'Iseran, France.

Left: 1.9 *Eritrichium nanum*, a high-altitude cushion plant of the forget-me-not family. Italian alps.

Left: 1.10 The hard cushions of this compressed member of the daisy family from New Zealand (*Raoulia eximea*), are known colloquially as 'vegetable sheep'.

Introduction

At the upper limit of plant life the low-growing plants, especially bryophytes (mosses and liverworts) and lichens, may dominate the flora. These simple, primitive plants, to which few of us give a second glance when plant hunting in high places, are especially well adapted to colonizing rock and bare ground. They are also more resistant than higher plants (that is, the more evolved seed-producing plants) to intense insolation, cold and desiccation. Perhaps these unassuming plants should be regarded as the ultimate alpines!

Species richness generally decreases with elevation, falling off sharply towards the upper limit of vegetation (**Figure 1.1**). The reasons for this are not adequately researched but appear to be combinations of several factors: the reduced biodiversity (species richness) generally associated with less productive habitats (**Figure 1.2**); the frequency of soil disturbance (limiting the range of habitat niches), and the limitations to cross pollination imposed by the scarcity of insect pollinators, with reduced opportunities for hybridization (and eventually the development of new species) as a result.

On a local scale, at least, there is no obvious latitudinal gradient in species richness among high mountain and tundra communities: temperate mountains have comparable diversity to those of tropical alpine areas (Wade and McVean 1969). This is in striking contrast to the clear latitudinal gradient in diversity generally found among lowland plant communities, where species numbers generally decline with increased distance from the equator.

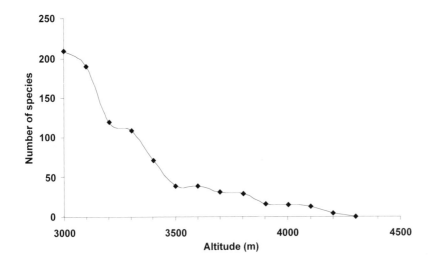

Figure 1.1
Species richness versus elevation.

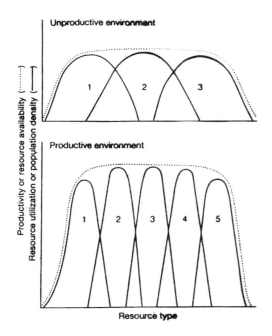

Figure 1.2
Site productivity versus
species richness and
abundance.

Rates of plant colonization and succession (the development of communities) on bare ground following disturbance are generally slow in mountains, compared with the lowlands. At low elevations succession on bare soils generally involves invasion by early successional specialist species (often annuals or biennials). These disappear later in succession, and are replaced by longer-lived late successional species. This sequence of events can be easily observed in a neglected vegetable garden that is overrun by annual weeds.

Early successional specialists – pioneer plants – generally decline in importance with increasing elevation. Succession takes the form of a gradual accumulation of species that persist as a mature community. This often results in the formation of mosaics of multi-species separated by bare ground. These gradually coalesce to form more-or-less complete cover if the soil remains undisturbed. All these successional processes are affected by a wide range of factors that will be explained further as they arise throughout this book.

Geology is important in determining abundance and diversity of alpine vegetation. The reasons are partly physical: softer, more easily weathered rocks, which are often sedimentary (such as limestone, sandstone or shale), tend to produce a greater range of habitat niches than harder, more durable igneous or metamorphic rocks (such as granite, pelite or basalt). Some rocks also decompose more readily, providing deeper, more fertile soils. The other main factor is the pH of the soil. It is a well known fact that some plants grow naturally only on acidic or alkaline formations. In addition, alkaline soils are inherently more productive than acidic soils; because the rate of nutrient cycling is faster, these soils can be exploited by a wider range of species. Chapters 6 and 7 provide a more thorough analysis of the influence of geology and soils, and the associated influence of nutritional indicators on alpine plant distributions and abundance.

The ultimate *raison d'être* of all living things is reproduction, and alpine plants have evolved many mechanisms for passing on their genes to future generations. Sexual reproduction is the most effective mechanism for ensuring long-term survival of a species. This is because the mixing of genetic material from two parents creates combinations in the offspring that have not previously existed, and these can be acted upon by natural selection as environmental conditions change. A kind of natural selection, albeit assisted, also occurs in the garden, and is one of the main reasons why many species become easier to grow after a few generations have been raised sequentially from seed. Only those seedlings that can cope with conditions experienced in the seed pan, when pricked out, and subsequently in the garden (or a pot, if an alpine house plant) survive; these go on to reproduce in turn, and so may remain in cultivation.

Despite the advantages of sexual reproduction, many alpines reproduce primarily by asexual reproduction, without any re-combination of genetic material. In severe mountain environments, where seedling survival may be unreliable, an increase by vegetative means such as fragmentation, production of bulbils or production of seed without fertilization (apomixis) is more likely to succeed. In these terms asexual reproduction is more energy-efficient than sexual reproduction, where most seed is wasted by failing to reach a suitable germinations site, not germinating if it does or dying before reaching sexual maturity. These and other aspects of alpine plant reproduction are discussed in Chapter 8.

There is great variability in species richness among alpine plant communities. For example, the alpine flora of the northern Andes has many more genera (more than 300), and from more plant families, than the floras of the smaller and more fragmented alpine areas of east Africa (103 genera) and Papua New Guinea (107 genera) that lie at a similar latitude. Variations in habitat area and isolation during the glacial-interglacial cycles of the last 2 million years appear to be particularly important in determining species richness in areas substantially affected by those events. These variations also explain some of the puzzling disjunct distributions of closely related plant genera and species. For example, *Kalmiopsis leachiana* (found in Oregon) and *Rhodothamnus chamaecistus* (found in the European Alps) are visually similar and inter-fertile. Likewise, very similar farinose primulas are found in North America and the extreme south of South America, but not in between, while *Gentiana pyrenaica* occurs in the Pyrenees (**Plate 1.12**) and the Carpathians, but not in the Alps. Chapter 9 provides more information on the factors influencing the origin and present distribution of arctic-alpine floras.

Left: 1.12 *Gentiana pyrenaica* has a disjunct distribution, occurring (as here) in the Pyrenees and the Carpathians but not in the Alps.

When considering plant distributions, it has to be remembered that even where a species or group of allied species from widely separated mountain areas look very similar, they may in fact be very different physiologically. This is because the plants from a particular mountain region must be able to cope with the often very specific local environmental conditions. Transplanted from their 'home' mountains into what would appear to be suitable conditions on another, distant mountain they might well be poorly suited to the different conditions and unable to survive. For similar reasons, plants raised from seed of a particular species from one mountain group may be easier to cultivate in gardens in a particular climatic zone than those raised from seed of the same species that were collected elsewhere. This is why it is important not to adopt a 'stamp collector' mentality, where once a plant (or seed of that plant) has been obtained, it is ticked off one's wish list. The wise alpine gardener seeks constantly to enhance the genetic variability within his or her collection by both growing plants from seed collected in different wild locations and exchanging plants and seed with fellow enthusiasts. This is especially important when, as is now certain, the climate of the earth is changing. The retreat of glaciers in most of the world's mountains vividly illustrates the gathering pace of global warming, with reliable current predictions indicating there will be no glaciers left in either the European Alps, the Antipodes, or in Japan by 2050. Alpine plants generally find it difficult to compete with plants from lower elevations. It is likely they will come under severe pressure as their alpine habitat diminishes and lowland plants move up the mountains. This is already happening in the Alps and probably elsewhere. But where the

availability of potential new alpine habitat higher up is limited by relatively low maximum elevation (for instance, in the Apennines of Italy, the Atlas Mountains of Morocco and the Olympic Mountains of the American Pacific North-west – see **Plate 1.13**), alpine plant communities are likely to be replaced. This will cause many species to be lost. This alarming prospect is considered in more detail in Chapter 10.

By understanding as much as possible about the origins of plants that are successful or unsuccessful in our gardens, and acquiring a detailed knowledge of the local habitats from which they originate, we may improve our ability to cultivate not only these species but also other plants from the same or similar locations. This does not mean that we should try to replicate natural conditions precisely – to do so would be difficult in most cases, if not impossible, and beyond the finances of most of us. But knowing whether a plant comes from an environment that is dry during much of the growing season rather than wet, or provides reliable winter snow cover or not, is characterized by extreme diurnal temperature fluctuations or is relatively temperate, or has acid or alkaline soils – this kind of knowledge is very helpful in honing our horticultural skills, as well as being intrinsically fascinating to the keen grower.

Above: 1.13 Alpines inhabiting mountain ranges with modest maximum elevations, such as the Olympic Mountains of Washington State, USA, which peak at only approximately 2,500 metres (8,000 feet), are particularly vulnerable to climate warming. This is because there are few opportunities for them to move upwards and thus escape competition from the more vigorous lowland species.

2·ARCTIC AND ALPINE ECOSYSTEMS

Professional ecologists, when asked to list the ten most important ecological concepts, ranked the ecosystem concept first (Cherrett 1989). The concept, a simple one, is that living organisms interact in a dynamic way, both with each other and with the non-living components of the ecosystem within which they exist. This implies that the ecosystem is 'more than the sum of its parts'.

While the ecosystem concept is of central importance to ecology, you may be wondering why it should form the basis of a book on the ecology of alpine plants, and one intended primarily for alpine gardeners. But by considering plants in relation to the ecosystems in which they grow naturally, you are likely to enhance your understanding of what makes them 'tick'. This understanding should make you a better grower, and will perhaps add a new dimension to your enjoyment of alpines. Adopting the ecosystem approach is particularly appropriate for alpine gardening which, unlike most branches of horticulture, is still concerned primarily with the cultivation of wild species, rather than garden hybrids and cultivars. Since we often grow alpines from seed collected in the mountains, it makes common sense to compare the growing conditions we are able to contrive in the garden with the alpine ecosystems that the plants have evolved to cope with and naturally inhabit.

Seeing alpines in their natural mountain environment, we are confronted by many questions that are fundamentally ecological in nature. Why is the tree line in the mountains generally so even and abrupt? How are alpines able to survive and reproduce in such hostile environments? How important an influence is snow to alpine plant distributions? Are pests and pathogens really absent from alpine habitats, as is often suggested and, if they are not, why are high alpines so susceptible to pests and diseases in the garden? When attempting answers to such questions, it helps to think of the plants in relation to their environment – as part of an alpine ecosystem that is formed from an interaction of living and non-living components. This complex web is the totality within which alpine plants live and reproduce.

Ecosystems

An ecosystem is a natural system in which a community of organisms interacts with its non-living environment. Thus alpine ecosystems contain not only alpine plants, but all the other living organisms present, as well as the components of soil, water and atmosphere that support and interact with them. The ecosystem as a concept is not limited by scale or extent but, for practical purposes, the most useful scale for us is the plant community and its immediate environment (alpine meadow, scree, bog, rock ledge etc.). By understanding the various relationships between alpine plants and the other components of their ecosystem, we not only increase our chances of growing alpines well in our gardens, but add a new dimension to our appreciation of them.

A major advantage of the ecosystem as a concept is that it is not fundamentally limited by scale or extent. So we can (although it is perhaps unusual to do so) choose to regard an individual plant, in its immediate natural environment, as a mini-ecosystem. With this in mind we may investigate how this plant arrived in its environment, how it manages to survive, how it is affected by the soil in which it grows or by its neighbours – and how it affects them, in turn. Moving up in our scale of observations, and more conventionally, we can next consider the ecosystem of the alpine meadow, or scree, or rock ledge of which this individual plant forms a part. Next in the hierarchy comes the alpine ecosystem as a whole, which includes alpine meadows (**Plate 2.1**), bogs (**Plate 2.2**), screes (**Plate 2.3**), rock crevices (**Plate 2.4**), alpine streams (**Plate 2.5**) and lakes (**Plate 2.6**). And at the final level of the global ecosystem, alpine ecosystems – along with forest, grassland, desert, marine and all other ecosystems – form part of the encompassing biosphere (the surface of the Earth).

Opposite page

Top left: 2.3 Mobile and stabilized limestone scree. Vrsc Pass, Slovenia.
Top right: 2.4 *Campanula zoysii* growing in a limestone rock crevice. Slovenia.
Bottom left: 2.6 Alpine lake. Lago de la Ercina, Covadonga, Picos de Europa, Spain.
Bottom right: 2.5 Alpine stream. Pyrenees.

Below left: 2.1 Alpine meadow on limestone soil. Pordoi Pass, Dolomites.
Below right: 2.2 Bog vegetation growing in a springline seepage. Pyrenees.

Characteristics of Ecosystems

By definition, ecosystems must contain living organisms, although not all ecosystems contain higher plants or vertebrate animals. And living organisms, through their processes of circulation, transformation and the accumulation of energy and matter, are central to the ecosystem's functioning. Microorganisms play a key role in these processes, but higher plants, where present, also play a part. But in order for plants to survive, grow and reproduce, the ecosystem must supply everything that is necessary for these processes to take place: the essential requirements are energy, water, carbon dioxide and oxygen, as well as macro-elements such as nitrogen, phosphorus and potassium and micro-elements that are required in smaller amounts.

While the alpine ecosystem provides all the essential raw materials of life, and thus provides an ideal plant habitat, one has to remember the severity of alpine climates, with their seasonal, even diurnal, temperature extremes. Also, a successful plant not only has to take root and grow but must also compete satisfactorily with others of its own kind, as well as with other species that are trying, equally hard, to acquire resources. In order to have the potential to reproduce, it must at least hold its own or, ideally, dominate and outgrow its neighbours. It must be able to survive the attacks of pests and diseases, either by resisting them, perhaps by developing a thick cuticle or spines, or by producing substances that make it unpalatable (even though the latter uses up precious energy). Alternatively, the plant may tolerate the depredations of pests and diseases, and use the energy saved for producing extra growth, allowing it to grow faster than it can be 'eaten'. Most plants have evolved a compromise response, involving an element of both defence and regrowth. By surviving competitors, pests and diseases the plant, through reproduction, can pass on more of its genes to succeeding generations – the *raison d'être* of all living things.

Alpine environments are not only harsh; they are among the most dynamic on Earth. At first sight instability, a characteristic common to most alpine ecosystems, seems only to add to the problems encountered by alpine plants. They are liable to be subjected not only to wildly fluctuating climatic extremes, but to rapid and unpredictable physical disruption. Rock falls, avalanches and the 'flash' floods that follow rapid snowmelt can each sweep away, in minutes, ecosystems that had developed over decades or even centuries. On the flanks of volcanoes, such as those in the Cascades of North America and in the Andes, all life can be obliterated by eruptions, as was demonstrated so dramatically by the explosive disintegration of the north flank of Mount St Helens in 1980. It is easy to

24

Left: 2.7 Sub-alpine pine wood with *Hepatica nobilis*. Grand Canyon du Verdon, France.

Below: 2.8 Alpine meadow on conglomerate soil. Ostafa, Italian Alps.

underestimate this dynamic characteristic of alpine ecosystems, particularly since most plant enthusiasts usually visit the mountains in summer, when conditions are relatively stable. The full magnitude of disturbance only becomes apparent if one visits the same area in winter as well as summer, and repeatedly over a number of years.

The dynamic nature of alpine plant communities is most obvious in the case of scree and other mobile habitats, but even in relatively stable, long-established habitats, such as sub-alpine woodland (**Plate 2.7**) and alpine meadow (**Plate 2.8**), the pageant of flowers, while perhaps having a fairly constant cast of species, is ever changing. Individuals of the same or different species may come and go, taking advantage of disturbance caused by animals, and the space created by the death of their predecessors or neighbours. But in general, while alpine ecosystems are dynamic, they are also resilient – able to absorb changes and still persist. If this were not the case, we would not recognize particular ecosystems as being distinct and different from others.

For some types of ecosystem resilience depends, paradoxically, on change. A good example is the alpine scree, which if not disturbed from time to time may eventually become an alpine meadow. Examples of this successional process are shown in **Plate 2.9** and **Plate 2.10**. Far from being disadvantaged by disturbance, true scree plants are favoured by it. Often short-lived as individuals, scree plants characteristically reproduce by vegetative fragmentation (for example, in many campanulas and sedums), or have deep-delving taproots that can produce new shoots after decapitation once the scree resettles (as in many members of the dandelion and cabbage families). In the closed community of the alpine meadow, where the ability to compete successfully for resources is paramount, these scree plants are generally unable to compete and soon die out. Other alpine ecosystems, such as rock crevices, are relatively stable compared with screes. Species which grow in these more stable ecosystems are less resilient to disturbance and are generally poor competitors who require their own bit of space. However, once established, individual crevice plants are often comparatively long-lived.

Far left: 2.9 Mobile screes with a scattering of plants. Mt Kuhtai, Austria.

Left: 2.10 Stabilized scree (in background) with alpine meadow community, stabilized scree in foreground. Dolomites.

Scree

Scree is a landform characteristic of mountainous areas where night temperatures frequently fall below 0°C (32°F), but are above freezing at other times. It is not generally found in arctic-alpine regions, where temperatures are invariably low. Water freezes within cracks in the rock at night and during winter, thawing again with the subsequent rise in temperature. Ice expands as it forms, and repetition of the freeze-thaw process gradually widens the cracks, eventually causing the rock to break. Debris falls down to the base of the crags forming, over time, a steep apron of scree.

Scree comprises angular fragments of rock, compositionally the same as the crags from which they originally came. The landform is typically concave and steepest at the top, with a maximum angle of around 40°. The central, and longest, part of the scree lies at angles between 25° and 33°, and the lowest part may be at quite a shallow angle. The steepest screes are formed from large polygonal blocks of rock such as granite or limestone, whereas platy fragments of mudstone or 'slate' form the shallowest slopes. Large blocks are commonly seen at the base of the landform. The surface of the scree is characteristically a very open structure, particularly where fragments are large and polygonal. Beneath this, space between fragments is much reduced by the sieving of smaller fragments through the surface cavities and through the breakdown by chemical weathering of weaker rock fragments. Space is much reduced deep inside the deposit core and parts may contain much fine material – particularly in screes dominated by mudstone, which weathers very readily. Internally, screes may be bedded parallel to the slope (**Plate 2.11**). Scree deposits are probably no thicker than 10-15 metres (33-49 feet).

Very extensive screes, up to 500 metres (1,600 feet) high, are typical in the Himalayas, for example. In the mountains of Britain, screes mostly formed after the last glaciers melted and, though a few active ones remain – for example at Wastwater in the Lake District, England – many have now been stabilized by vegetation. Accumulations of rock talus, with a scree-like structure but generally composed of larger fragments, occur commonly alongside roads in mountainous areas.

Left: 2.11 Cross-section through a scree showing the internal bedded structure

Thus, different species of alpine plants have different niches within particular kinds of alpine ecosystems to which they have become particularly well adapted by evolution. Within their own niches, which may be very limited in the cases of the most specialized species, alpine plants can compete with all comers. But elsewhere, even perhaps nearby, they may have no chance of survival. Some of the cushion dionysias have become adapted through evolution to survive in situations where few other plants could grow – upside down in limestone caves, where they never receive direct precipitation. They can compete there, but nowhere else. Arctic-alpine cushion plants such as *Saxifraga hypnoides* flourish at sea level in the narrow limestone crevices (grikes) in the limestone pavement of the Burren in the west of Ireland (**Plate 2.12**). But they would have no chance of survival in the adjacent limestone grassland among the daisies and dandelions. So alpines, like all plants of extreme environments, succeed in growing where they do because they have evolved as specialists, able to tolerate conditions that eliminate or control the competition. But this does not mean they are unable, physiologically, to grow in less harsh conditions – if they were, we could not cultivate them in our gardens.

Left: 2.12 *Saxifraga hypnoides* growing in limestone pavement at sea level on the Burren in Co. Clare, Ireland.

Rock Crevices

Crevices are rock structures that have been widened by surface weathering: the structures are sedimentary layering or bedding, joints and faults **(Plate 2.13)**, cleavage in slate and a marked planar foliation (leaf-like layers) in metamorphic rocks. The presence and intensity of these structures determine the form of the rock exposures.

Bedding

Sedimentary rocks such as sandstone, mudstone and limestone occur in beds, successive layers built up from episodes of sediment settling. Beds may be thick – measured in metres – or thin – on a millimetre scale. The parallel boundaries separating beds are called bedding planes. Weathering along these planes produces narrow cracks, and some rocks split along these surfaces. Cross-bedding may be formed by flowing water moulding sediment into ripples; by changing river currents cutting and redepositing sediment in channels, or by the wind forming dunes. Sediment containing mixed sizes of grain forms graded bedding; the larger, heavier particles settle faster than the smaller ones, and repeated influxes of sediment will produce a distinctive pattern, with the larger particles at the base of each bed. Though most sedimentary rocks were deposited on flat or very gently inclined surfaces, many have been tilted and folded subsequently by Earth processes. Metamorphic rocks such as gneiss and schist have a layering or foliation, similar to bedding. This is formed by the parallel orientation of newly crystallized minerals such as mica, created as a result of intense heat and compression deep in the Earth's crust.

Left: 2.13 The continuous layering inclined gently to the right is bedding and the near vertical fractures are joints. Note that both are through-going structures. St Bees, Cumbria.

Joints and faults

These are fractures in the Earth's crust produced by stresses, and can happen in all rocks. Joints are fractures with no relative movement across them, whereas faults have displacement. Joints are a very common type of crevice for plants . Well-jointed sedimentary rocks are commonly divided into rectangular blocks by two sets of joints, in addition to the bedding; these structures are approximately at right angles to each other (**Plate 2.14**). Most joints traverse a considerable thickness of strata and, in some rocks, are regularly and widely spaced, making them suitable for building stone. In others they are so closely spaced that the rock breaks up into small pieces. Within the interior of the rock mass joints are tightly closed, but at the surface they are widened by both the release of stresses and weathering.

Cleavage

Cleavage is a very regular and closely spaced set of nearly vertical fractures that is characteristic of slate, which splits readily along these planes into thin sheets (**Plate 2.15**). Cleavage was formed through intense compression of fine-grained sedimentary rocks, such as mudstone, when they were buried deep in the Earth's crust during mountain building. Weathering weakens the rock along the cleavage, typically producing sharp slabs protruding from the ground. Slate is typically abundant in the older mountain belts, such as the Caledonides of Scandinavia and northern Britain, and in the Tien Shan of Central Asia.

Above: 2.14 The sandstone is cut by two, near-straight joint sets at c. 90° to each other; the flat slab inclined towards the viewer is bedding. St Bees, Cumbria.

Above left: 2.15 *Juniperus communis* exploiting crevices developed along cleavage. Hope Beck, Lake District, England.

3·SURVIVAL, GROWTH AND DEVELOPMENT

Life Forms of Alpine Plants

Terrestrial plants of arctic and high altitude alpine regions are mainly flowering plants (angiosperms), bryophytes (mosses and liverworts) and lichens. Ferns are also represented, but with fewer species. Bryophytes and lichens are able to persist at altitudes and in environmental extremes where no higher plants can grow; this is because of their ability, most marked in the lichens, to withstand prolonged and extreme desiccation. Mosses tend to dominate in and below snowbanks, while lichens cling to the windswept, rocky barrens. Most of the flowering plants are perennial herbs or graminoids (grasses and their relatives), with usually a few very low-growing shrubs; annuals and biennials, tall shrubs and plants with underground storage organs are uncommon. A typical representation is provided in **Table 3.1**, which shows the proportions of these differing life forms in the high altitude flora of the Hindu Kush, Afghanistan.

Altitude range in metres (feet)	Tall shrubs	Dwarf shrubs/ thorny cushions	Perennial herbs and graminoids	Bulbs, rhizomes, tubers etc	Biennials	Annuals
>5,400 (17,700)	-	10	70	10	10	-
5,200-5,400 (17,000-17,700)	-	16	74	5	5	-
5,000-5,200 (16,400-17,000)	-	12	71	4	8	6
4,800-5,000 (15,700-16,400)	-	12	72	4	6	5
4,500-4,800 (14,800-15,700)	2	12	69	7	4	7
4,000-4,500 (13,100-14,800)	3	17	61	7	2	9

Table 3.1: Life forms as proportions (%) of the total alpine flora in zones above 4,000 metres (13,100 feet) altitude in the Hindu Kush Mountains. (Breckle, cited in Körner 1999)

Life forms

Mosses, liverworts and lichens are perhaps the archetypal plants of arctic and alpine regions because they are better able to withstand the extreme environmental conditions than higher plants. Nevertheless, flowering plants, most of them herbaceous perennials or very low shrubs, occur in all but the most inhospitable sites. Annuals and biennials are uncommon because annuals must succeed in completing the whole life cycle, from seed germination to seed production on a yearly basis, and biennials must accomplish the same over two years – a precarious task in such severe environments. On the other hand, perennials need only produce viable seed occasionally in order to pass on their genes.

Prostrate shrubs are generally the longest-lived alpines, although not usually dominant in alpine plant communities, either in terms of species diversity or overall abundance. In some cases (for example, *Kelseya uniflora*) they may not look like shrubs at all, but rather resemble long-lived, non-woody cushion plants (such as *Silene acaulis*). They often grow very slowly, only able to allocate a very small amount of precious carbon to their permanent woody structures each year.

Most of the herbaceous perennials in alpine communities are grasses, leafy dicotyledons or cushion dicotyledons. Monocotyledons (including most bulbs) are uncommon, except in hot and/or dry mountains, where they have the advantage of being protected from water loss below ground during summer.

There is only one annual species, *Koenigia islandica*, in the high Arctic (beyond the 80th parallel). Interestingly, as well as being circumpolar in the Northern Hemisphere this species also occurs in Tierra del Fuego, at the southernmost tip of South America. (For a map of its distribution, and that of other widely distributed arctic-alpines, see Love and Love 1974. See also Chapter 9 for a detailed discussion of why some alpine plants occur in disjunct distributions.)

Annuals are only slightly more common in temperate mountains: for example, on the Beartooth Plateau of Wyoming only three out of a total of 191 species of flowering plants were found to be annuals (Johnson and Billings 1962). Between 1 and 2 per cent of annuals seems to be about the norm in these environments, while in temperate lowland grassland ecosystems the figure is typically 10 per cent or more.

Some species that are normally annuals when growing near the tree line, and are listed as annuals in floras, may occur in perennial form at higher elevations. Thus, in the Medicine Bow Mountains of Wyoming all plants of *Androsace septentrionalis* at 2,000 metres (6,600 feet) elevation were annual, but at 3,640 metres (11,900 feet) at least 80 per cent of the same species were found to be perennial. Knowledge of such naturally occurring ecotypic variation should cause judges at alpine flower shows to think twice before disqualifying a plant from consideration, simply because the floras say it is normally an annual, and annuals are not according to schedule; it might well be a perennating form.

Annual and biennial plants are scarce in tundra environments, principally because the short, cold growing season discourages a recurring reproductive cycle, while perennial plants have the advantage in that they do not need to reproduce annually and, in their early years, can put all their efforts into vegetative growth. After this, perennials need only set seed occasionally to ensure that the species survives and that, as individuals, they contribute their genes to future generations. The differing strategies of biennial and perennial species are exemplified by a study of the reproductive biology of gentians in the White Mountains of California (Spira and Pollak 1986). The biennial species (G. *tenella*, G. *prostrata*) were characterized by their production of large numbers of fruits, each containing many seeds. By contrast, fruit and seed set were considerably less and yearly seed production relatively low in the perennial G. *newberryi*. Closer analysis revealed that the biennial species allocated a much larger proportion of their resources to flower, fruit and seed production than the perennial. Also, while G. *newberryi* depended on cross-pollination, which was often unreliable, G. *tenella* and G. *prostrata* relied on the more dependable mechanism of self-pollination.

Prostrate shrubs, defined as having permanent woody or sub-woody structure, exhibit the permanence of perenniality to the highest degree of any alpine plants, generally living longer than herbaceous perennials. So powerful are the environmental factors controlling form in arctic and alpine plants that the dwarf tundra shrubs often closely resemble non-woody cushion plants. Compare, for example, the sub-shrub *Azorella monantha* (**Plate 3.1**) with the herbaceous cushion plant *Silene acaulis* (**Plate 3.2**). Both are equally congested and have similar small narrow leaves and stemless flowers. These very congested dwarf shrubs often grow extremely slowly and so require very little energy input (in the form of carbohydrate produced by photosynthesis) in order to survive from year to year. This, as well as other characteristics – notably their tolerance of extreme cold –

enables such shrubs as *Cassiope tetragona* and *Salix arctica* to grow almost at the northern limit of vegetation in the Arctic; both species extend north of latitude 83° in northern Greenland (Holmen 1957).

Despite the benefits of the dwarf shrub habit the majority of vascular plants in arctic and alpine environments are herbaceous perennials. These are of three main kinds: grasses, leafy dicotyledons and cushion dicotyledons. A few monocotyledons with bulbs or other underground storage organs also occur, and these tend to increase in relative importance in the flora of the hotter, drier mountain ranges where retirement below ground in summer (aestivation) is an effective means of

Above left: 3.1 Cushion of the sub-shrub *Azorella monantha* growing among rocks in the central Andes of Argentina.

Above right: 3.2 *Silene acaulis* (a non-woody cushion plant) shows the same habit as *Azorella monantha* (see Plate 3.1), hugging the rock to avoid wind chill and conserve heat and moisture.

Left: 3.3 In areas with hot, dry summers, bulbs such as *Tulipa doerfleri* form a significant component of montane vegetation. Kedros Mountains, Crete.

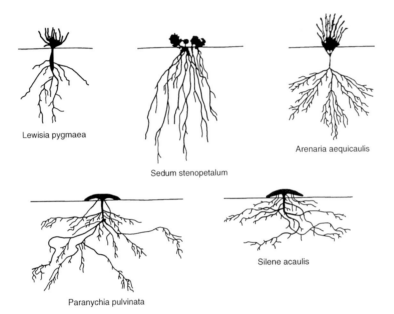

Lewisia pygmaea

Sedum stenopetalum

Arenaria aequicaulis

Silene acaulis

Paranychia pulvinata

Left: Figure 3.1 Morphology of alpines showing different root and shoot formations.

combating drought (**Plate 3.3**). Typically, the dicotyledons have a deep primary root system, with shoots proliferating near the soil surface and no clear main stem (**Figure 3.1**). A few species have underground storage organs, such as swollen roots (for example, *Lewisia* spp., *Weldenia candida*) or rhizomes (as in many gentians, campanulas and primulas) that are utilized in food storage.

At the altitudinal limit for vascular plants to grow in the mountains there is a greater variety of form in the less harsh environment of the snowbeds than on the windswept ridges and rock outcrops. The snowbed vegetation typically comprises grasses, small herbs, cushion plants and dwarf shrubs such as *Salix herbacea*. On the exposed areas, small-leaved dwarf rosette plants and moss-like or cushion plants predominate, with occasional grass tussocks. Such well-loved species as *Silene acaulis*, *Saxifraga oppositifolia* and *Dryas octopetala* are common in these most extreme environments. McGraw (1985) compared ecotypes (members of a species) of *Dryas octopetala* collected from open ridges and snowbeds at the same elevation. He found that when both types were grown together under 'lush' conditions (with high nutrient and light levels and high water availability) the snowbed plants were larger in all their parts and also better withstood competition from other plants of either ecotype. In contrast, the plants from the open habitat were

Left: 3.4 *Saxifraga biflora* is a typical high-altitude snowbed species. Col de L'Iseran, French Alps.

particularly poorly equipped to cope with root competition but were more tolerant of extreme temperatures and high wind speeds than the snowbed plants. These differences show how natural selection can promote different ecotypes within a single species, and over a very small geographical range when selection pressures are strong enough.

On the highest rocky peaks, where most of the ground remains snow-free and exposed to the fierce cold in winter, there are miniature 'snowbeds' in the rock crevices that provide havens for snowbed species otherwise found only at lower elevations. The snow provides high-altitude specialists such as *Ranunculus glacialis* with both winter shelter and, in the short growing season, a supply of water – albeit at close to freezing temperatures. These high-altitude snowbed plants depend upon meltwater to a greater extent than most alpines so they must be able to grow with their roots continually bathed in very cold water. In many cases, though 'softer' in appearance than the moss-like or cushion plants of exposed ridges and rock crevices, they are able – through the protection provided by snow cover – to reach higher elevations. They extend well up into the zone of permanent snow, where their only associates are crustose lichens and a few moss tufts. *Saxifraga biflora* (**Plate 3.4**), a typical snowbed species, holds the altitude record in the Alps at 4,400 metres (14,400 feet), closely followed by *Androsace alpina*, which reaches 4,270 metres (14,000 feet) on the Finsteraarhorn (Swiss Alps). *Ranunculus glacialis* holds the altitude record in the Arctic where it has been found growing at 2,370 metres (7,700 feet) on Galdhøpiggen in Norway. A similar and interesting parallel case occurs in New Zealand where another buttercup, *Ranunculus grahamii*, similarly an unlikely looking candidate to hold records for growing at high elevations, survives in snow crannies well above the permanent snow at 2,900 metres (9,500 feet) on Malte Brun. Only two other species of flowering plants, *Parahebe birleyi* and *Hebe haastii*, grow higher in the New Zealand mountains. Both of these are also snow cranny plants, whose straggly appearance belies their ability to survive in such extreme habitats.

Left: 3.5 Diverse Paramo vegetation with typical tall rosette *Espeletia* sp. (*Asteraceae*) and *Puya* sp. (*Bromeliaceae*). Colombian Andes.

Left: 3.6 *Senecio brassica* has large cabbage-like rosettes that protect the vulnerable crown during freezing tropical nights. Mt Kenya.

Tropical mountain vegetation is quite different, floristically, from the arctic-alpine types described so far, and much more complex. Tropical alpines, such as the giant lobelias and groundsels found in the mountains of eastern Africa, and the espeletias, puyas and lupins in the Andes (**Plate 3.5**), are often columnar or sub-arborescent in form. In addition, they sometimes have large woolly leaves that fold inwards over the growing crown during the freezing tropical nights and spread out to capture moisture and sunlight during the day (**Plate 3.6**).

Growers of high alpines are already aware that these plants tend to have proportionately larger root systems than other garden plants, and this is also the case in the wild. When alpine plants are dug up and the soil carefully cleaned from the roots then dried, divided into roots and shoots, and weighed, the root:shoot ratios vary over a wide range from about 4:1 to 1:5 (excluding attached dead biomass, which may be considerable, especially in cushion plants). Values greater than 1:1 (indicating there is more root than shoot) are rarely found in plants from lowland ecosystems, with the exception of arid habitats where underground storage organs have evolved to protect the resting plant from desiccation. The importance of the large root systems of many arctic and alpine plants, apart from their role in anchoring the plants and obtaining water and nutrients, is mainly as carbohydrate stores. Roots provide reservoirs of energy that tide the plants through the long winter and then fuel the burst of growth that takes place in spring as soon as the snow and ice melts. This ability to grow and flower quickly when the soil temperature begins to rise, using stored food reserves, is a key characteristic of alpine plants. It allows them to persist and grow in environments with short growing seasons.

Root:shoot ratios

Alpines generally have a greater proportion of roots to shoots than most other plants, except xerophytes (such as cacti). Large root systems anchor the plants in exposed situations, allow them to obtain sufficient water and nutrients from often skeletal soils and serve as essential carbohydrate, or energy, stores. When cultivating high alpines it is important to try to maintain high root:shoot ratios by providing well-drained, airy composts that encourage root growth, and by potting on as soon as the pot is full of roots. Potting should only be done during the growing season because roots damaged or lost during repotting in late autumn or winter cannot be replaced. Also, when the plant is dormant it cannot take up more water than it has lost by passive transpiration; the moisture content of the soil should be reduced in winter to the minimum required to keep the plant healthy.

Since the over-wintering roots provide an important store of energy for early spring growth, it is important, when cultivating them, to ensure that the soil or compost in which they are growing remains neither too wet nor too dry during the dormant period, and that the roots are protected from prolonged freezing temperatures. Plants situated outside can be watered, if necessary, during periods of drought, protected from excessive rain with cloches or panes of glass or from freezing by the use of mulches or cloches – or both. The roots of plants growing in pots, troughs and other containers are potentially more prone to drought, waterlogging and freezing, as well as to overheating in summer; the small volume of soil in which they are growing is not buffered from extremes, unlike the larger, continuous volume of soil in the garden. Thus in gardens with extreme climates plants in pots should be plunged in sand or some other insulating material at all times, while larger containers, including troughs, should be protected by whatever means are available or can be contrived.

It is inadvisable, as well as being generally unnecessary, to repot plants in the late autumn or winter; better that the plants be slightly pot bound during their annual period of dormancy, rather than risk root loss. Repotting at the traditional time, immediately after flowering when the plant is growing busily and building up its reserves for the following winter, makes ecological as well as gardening sense. It is essential that there is always plenty of water available to the roots at this stage to mimic the snowmelt or rainfall of the mountains in spring and that there is abundant light for photosynthesis. Once the season's new growth has finished, and any repotted plants have filled the soil with roots, it is probably best to keep the plants rather dry until the following spring (unless they are known to originate from an alpine environment that has abundant summer moisture). Keeping the soil on the dry side prevents root loss due to anoxia (lack of oxygen) and also helps to limit late-season 'soft' growth, which is vulnerable both to disease and cold in the winter. Such growth would not occur naturally in the mountains, where the return of winter is accompanied by a rapid drop in temperatures.

An environmental hazard sometimes faced by plants growing in areas with summer drought, to which they must adapt in order to survive, is fire – either wildfire or deliberate burning to improve the quality of grazing lands. Plants that have taproots, rhizomes or other underground food stores can survive a fire and go on to produce new rosettes. These will have a good chance of survival, as will those naturally weedy plants that can take advantage of the short-lived open ground that burning creates. In the northern Andes, *Werneria nubigena* is a widespread species that forms large patches in grassland by means of its spreading rhizomes. Robert Rolfe reports (in personal correspondence with the author) that this species seldom flowered profusely except in areas where the farmers had set fire to the hillside several months previously in order to improve the pasture. In such places it was one of few plants to have re-established, probably because it was quickly able to produce a fresh batch of leaves to replace those lost. It seemed to Rolfe that this species positively benefited from the ravages of fire, possibly because it becomes too congested in established grassland. He also noted that a report from Peru indicates that this species grows best where the turf is tightly grazed by rabbits, and goes on to suggest that grazing also induces a flush of new growth, similar to that caused by fire. Local increase in soil fertility as a result of burning or depositing dung may also be a factor.

Growth and Development of Alpines

Alpine plants generally have slow growth rates compared with their lowland counterparts. It might seem obvious that this would be the case since alpines grow in harsher environments. However, we know that they continue to grow at a slower rate in the garden, so it is worth investigating the reasons more closely.

Since over 75 per cent of the dry matter of plants is carbon, growth can only occur when the plant takes up more carbon as carbon dioxide from the atmosphere (through photosynthesis) than it loses through respiration. This indicates that there must be less 'spare' carbon available for growth in slow-growing alpine plants in comparison to more productive lowland species. This might be due to alpines having less carbon uptake, more carbon loss, or a combination of both. With regard to carbon uptake, there are various possibilities: the photosynthetic process might be less efficient in alpine plants; the proportion of the plant's biomass given over to photosynthesis (the leaves) might be less than in other plants, or the period during which photosynthesis takes place might be shorter in alpine plants. If higher rates of carbon loss were the norm in alpines by comparison with lowland plants, this might be due to them either possessing more efficient respiration or undergoing respiration during a longer part of the growing season than in other plants. I will now review the evidence for each of these possibilities, such as it is.

Photosynthesis

One essential requirement for successful plant adaptation to arctic and alpine environments is the development of a metabolic system that can capture, store and utilize energy at low temperatures and over short periods of time – typically 6-12 weeks compared with, say, 30-40 weeks at sea level in temperate regions. In the mountains, photosynthetic activity occurs throughout most of the snow-free period when the temperature during daylight exceeds 0°C (32°F), or even, in the case of some species, when it is below freezing. Thus Moser *et al.* (1977) and Pisek *et al.* (1967) found that *Ranunculus glacialis* and *Oxyria digyna* can carry on net photosynthesis (that is, produce a carbon fixation in excess of that being respired) at temperatures as low as –6°C (21°F). In comparison, the leaves of most temperate crop plants cannot replace carbon lost by respiration at temperatures below about +5°C (41°F). Low temperature photosynthesis is possible in alpines such as *Ranunculus glacialis* and *Oxyria digyna* because they are more capable of withstanding greater super-cooling of their cell contents than plants from lower altitudes: their cell sap remains liquid, and functional, at lower temperatures.

41

Super-cooling is achieved by the plant converting insoluble starch in its cells to soluble sugar and takes place during the cold hardening process as the temperature falls in autumn. The vital cell organelles are then protected from damage within this thick, sugary solution.

Photosynthesis

Alpines generally have only a few weeks in which to make all the food they need to grow, flower, ripen seed, produce flower buds for the following year and survive the winter. They make up for the short summer, to some extent, with an ability to photosynthesize at low or even sub-zero temperatures. At higher temperatures their photosynthetic capacity (ability to absorb carbon under optimum conditions) is similar to that of other plants. Overall photosynthetic rates (carbon fixed per unit area of leaf) are also similar but, because alpines generally have thicker leaves than other plants (except xerophytes such as cacti and halophytes, which are salt-tolerant), their rates of photosynthesis based on leaf dry mass (rather than leaf area) are lower than those of other plants. In effect this means that, under ideal growing conditions, an alpine with a particular leaf area will produce less carbohydrate by photosynthesis than a non-alpine with the same leaf area.

Net photosynthesis (the difference between the amount of carbon dioxide fixed by photosynthesis and that lost by respiration) varies throughout the growing season. It is relatively low in spring, because of high respiratory rates associated with renewed growth and flowering. Later, after shoot growth ceases and while seeds mature, net photosynthesis increases appreciatively, and the excess carbohydrate produced is stored in the plant's roots and shoots.

While alpine plants are able to perform photosynthesis at lower temperatures than plants of warmer environments, their photosynthetic capacity (their ability to absorb carbon from carbon dioxide in the air under optimum conditions of temperature, light, water and nutrients) is little different from that of other plants. Based on carbon accumulation per unit of leaf area, the overall rates of photosynthesis of alpines in their natural environment are also similar to, or slightly higher than, those of related lowland plants. Respiration rates also seem generally to be similar in both groups – while perhaps a little higher in the arctic-alpines, they are insufficiently so to explain their lower growth rate. One study, which compared six contrasting *Poa* grass species (two alpine, one sub-alpine and three lowland), found that while the alpine species had similar rates of photosynthesis per unit of leaf area to those from lower elevations, they had significantly *lower* rates of photosynthesis per unit of leaf dry mass (Atken *et al.* 1996). This discrepancy was due to the leaves of the alpine species being thicker than those of the lowland species. For alpine species growing in harsh environments there is an obvious advantage to having thicker, tougher leaves than their lowland counterparts. But such protection has to be 'paid for' by less efficient photosynthesis, since light is only absorbed through the leaf surfaces; less leaf area equates to less space on the 'factory floor' where photosynthesis takes place.

As indicated above, low temperature has been found to be relatively unimportant in limiting photosynthesis in alpines. The amount of sunlight the leaves receive is more significant. Though alpine plants are well adapted to carry on photosynthesis at low temperatures, they are predominantly open-ground plants that need high light intensities in order to photosynthesize effectively. However, in dry mountains, moisture in the surface layers of often poorly developed soil may be quickly lost on slopes facing the sun. Here, plants may benefit from moderate shade or relief effects, which reduce insolation and associated water loss. There are trade-offs between potential losses of sunlight energy and the gains possible from retention of soil water and reduced transpiration (Körner 1999).

Photosynthesis in alpine plants is not uniform throughout the growing season. Net photosynthesis is relatively low early in the season. This is because of high respiratory rates associated with rapid growth and flowering during, and immediately after, snowmelt. The plant uses excess carbohydrate produced during the previous summer to take advantage of the whole of the short growing season. Net photosynthesis increases later in the season, when flowering and shoot growth has largely ceased and any seed that has been set has begun to swell. The excess carbohydrate produced is stored away in the shoots, and especially the roots, for use during the following winter and spring, rather than being used simply to produce more foliage. Conservation of precious carbohydrate is enhanced by an adaptation that enables most but not all alpine plants to reduce their respiration rate sharply as temperature increases in summer. This is described in more detail below.

A common phenomenon in alpines is the speeding up, or telescoping, of developmental processes in plants that are released from snow cover relatively late in the summer. Plants released from snow early in the season take much longer to reach maturity, and have a longer photosynthetic season, than those of the same species that are released from snow later. Nevertheless, there is a minimum growing season required by all alpine plants in order to fix sufficient carbon to survive and reproduce. This seems to be 6-7 weeks. Longer growing periods than this allow plants to acquire more carbon than would be required for mere survival. The extra carbon can be used not only in growth, and perhaps in extra flower and seed production, but also to counter losses due to herbivores and diseases that might otherwise weaken or kill the plant.

Respiration

Much less is known about respiration in alpine plants than about photosynthesis; the latter is much easier to measure since it occurs only, or mainly, in leaves, and there is only one major process involved. Respiration occurs in all plant tissues but at differing rates, determined by the micro-environments associated with these tissues; the micro-climates of roots are normally very different from those of leaves and stems. Also, there are different sorts of respiration, occurring at different rates at different times, and in differing organs. With these difficulties, and the fact that most of the research work on respiration has been done on crop plants and trees rather than wild plants such as alpines, it is not surprising that there is still much to be learnt about respiration in alpines. Nevertheless, we can glean some useful pieces of information from what we do know.

Generally speaking, when alpines and lowland plants are grown together at low temperatures of around 10°C (50°F), alpine plants respire more rapidly. But when both types are grown at higher temperatures of around 20°C (68°F), alpines respire at similar rates to lowland plants. The low temperature difference is probably because alpine plants need to respire actively when air temperatures are low, particularly in spring, in order to utilize stored food materials for growth. Most alpines respond to increasing temperatures by respiring more rapidly, but after a period of exposure to higher temperatures they generally readjust their respiration rates downwards. This is necessary to protect the plants from an undue loss of carbon that would occur if high respiration rates were maintained through the summer. There is one group of alpines, however, that – crucially – is *unable* to adjust to high temperatures in this way. These alpines continue to respire at rapid rates indefinitely when maintained at high temperatures in cultivation. These are alpine species that are characteristically found growing at the highest elevations (such as *Saxifraga biflora* and *Ranunculus glacialis*). Since they never experience prolonged periods of high temperature in their natural environment, they have had no need to evolve, or retain, mechanisms that provide protection from the damaging effects of high respiration rates at high temperatures. As a result, when exposed to constant high temperatures in cultivation they are likely to use more carbon than they fix, inevitably leading to loss of carbon reserves and, ultimately, death (Larigauderie and Körner 1995).

Respiration
Respiration, unlike photosynthesis, occurs in all plant tissues, not just in leaves. Alpine plants generally respire more rapidly at low temperatures than other plants but at the same rate in summer. However, prolonged experimental exposure to high temperatures results in lowered respiration rates in most alpines, helping to conserve carbohydrates required for winter survival. But some high alpines are unable to do this, presumably because they never experience prolonged high temperatures in nature. As a consequence they may respire themselves to death in the heat of a lowland summer. Keeping them cool is the best way of preventing this, or alternatively try growing plants from seed collected at low elevations, which may be suited to warmer temperatures.

This inability to control respiration rates at markedly higher temperatures than they experience in the wild is probably one of the main reasons why the alpines that grow at the highest elevations are generally the most difficult to grow at lower elevations in cultivation. They simply respire themselves to death during hot summer weather. It is only by keeping them cool, for example in shaded and, where possible, air-conditioned glasshouses or plunge beds that one can hope to grow them satisfactorily.

However, for those of us limited to using shading to reduce temperatures, another problem arises: high alpines generally receive very intense solar radiation in their natural habitats, and anything less than full sunlight at lowland elevations seems like semi-darkness to them; the plants often becoming markedly drawn (etiolated) and out of character. This problem may perhaps best be addressed, where possible, by growing plants of extreme high alpines from seed collected at the *lowest* elevations at which these species grow. This is because individual plants growing at lower elevations are more likely to have the capacity to reduce their respiration rates in response to higher temperatures, and this trait will be passed on to at least some of their offspring.

Pests and Diseases of Alpine Plants

In addition to experiencing harsh environmental conditions, high alpines have to cope with pests and diseases. These have been covered in detail in a special AGS publication (Ellis *et al.* 1993) so will only be outlined here. Pests come in many forms and sizes, ranging from insects to molluscs, small mammals such as marmots (**Plate 3.7**) and large herbivores such as chamois, llamas, sheep and cattle (**Plate 3.8**). While little is known of the depredations of the smaller pests on alpine plants, it can be assumed that these take their toll, and that the plants have evolved means of resisting their attacks. They can resist by either employing various defences, such as thick waxy cuticle or spines (**Plate 3.9**), or stinging hairs (**Plate 3.10**) or chemicals that are either toxic or make the leaves unpalatable. Or they can use the energy that such defences would cost in greater (compensatory) growth. Many species have evolved compromise strategies, putting some energy into defence mechanisms and the remainder into growth. In addition, both small and large herbivores may be fooled by camouflage and so miss out on a potential meal: *Ranunculus parnassifolius* is almost invisible except when in flower on its native scree slopes, as is the rosulate violet, *Viola congesta*, in its cindery home in the Andes (**Plate 3.11**). Indeed, Dora Stafford discovered a new species of *Nototriche* in Peru by sitting on it, and then shuffling over to investigate what had provided her with such a soft landing! (Rolfe, in personal communication.) Should the camouflage fail, the violet has a thick taproot that is capable of regeneration if decapitated, and Rolfe noted that those rosettes that had been browsed by animals had new shoots coming from their mangled bases.

Plants are certainly not free from disease in the mountains, as careful observation reveals. In their natural habitat, cushions of plants such as androsaces or drabas are rarely as perfect, or as large, as the unblemished domes we see at the Shows.

Far left: 3.8 Damage caused to cushion of *Armeria maritime* by cattle. Picos de Europa, Spain.

Left: 3.9 A spiny *Nassauvia* species. Argentina.

Left: 3.7 Hoary marmot (*Marmota caligata*) is an important grazer among alpine vegetation. Mt Rainier, Washington State.

Left: 3.10 *Caiophora prieta* has stinging hairs. Cerro Cathedral, Argentina.

Left: 3.11 *Viola congesta* is very well camouflaged against the rocks, thus enabling it to evade the attention of grazing animals. Chile.

However, as **Plate 3.12** indicates, when disease takes hold in the wild, it is usually 'compartmentalized', with a clear demarcation between affected and healthy tissue. When disease strikes cultivated plants, there is usually no such compartmentalization of the damage (**Plate 3.13**) and infection proceeds without check. There are probably two main reasons why alpines are more vulnerable to infection in cultivation. Firstly, the range of disease-causing organisms the plants are exposed to in cultivation is different from that in the wild. Just as many isolated South American Indian tribes have been wiped out by diseases such as measles, to which they have no natural immunity, so plants brought into cultivation may have no natural defences against diseases they would never encounter in the wild. Secondly, even if a plant has some potential resistance to a particular disease it may still not be able to deploy this resistance effectively in the garden because of the very different growing conditions there compared with in the wild. For both these reasons it is often necessary to give cultivated plants a helping hand by controlling pests and diseases. This is best done by providing growing conditions that encourage healthy growth although, from time to time, chemical assistance may also be required. When the need to use the latter arises it is generally advisable to proceed cautiously, especially in the case of seedlings or young plants, and use a more dilute chemical solution than recommended for more robust plants, for which these products are generally marketed. Another sensible precaution is not to treat all the plants of a particular species or cultivar at the same time – especially if it is a rarity.

Above left: 3.12 *Androsace helvetica* with 'compartmentalized' fungal infection. Schilthorn, Swiss Alps.

Above right: 3.13 Uncontrolled fungal pathogen rapidly killing a cushion of *Dionysia tapetodes*.

4·CLIMATE

Climate is the most obvious factor to affect both the growth of alpine plants in the wild, and the ease or difficulty of cultivating them in the garden. The principal climatic factors affecting plants are temperature, precipitation and irradiation.

Temperature

Sub-polar and alpine environments share important characteristics, but also differ substantially. What they have in common, primarily, is severe climate – especially cold, or cool, summers. Cold winters occur in other regions, such as the great central continental plains of North America and Eurasia, but the summers, as in both of these areas, may be hot. The significance of cold temperatures in summer becomes apparent to anyone who visits the high mountains. One soon learns to prepare for that sudden change from 'summer' to 'winter', as the clouds gather, covering the sun, the wind blows and a sudden shower of driving sleet chills to the bone. Even on days that are consistently bright, there is a very sharp drop in temperature as daylight begins to fade, and a high probability of frost at night. A study of climate in the fell field (alpine meadow) habitat of high-altitude, wind-exposed cushion communities (**Plate 4.1**) in New Zealand, revealed that the mean annual air temperature was close to freezing. Over a five-year period of continuous temperature recording at 1,590 metres (5,220 feet) in the Old Man Range, Central Otago, the longest period without frost was thirteen days. On average, over a year only about 20 per cent of the days were frost free, while on 30 per cent of days there was no thaw (Mark and Adams 1979). In such areas, *Dracophyllum muscoides* (**Plate 4.2**), a cushion-forming shrub in a genus that comprises mostly larger shrubs and small trees, often forms the dominant vegetation.

Below left: 4.1 Exposed high-altitude cushion plant community in Central Otago, South Island, New Zealand.

Below right: 4.2 *Dracophyllum muscoides* is a prominent member of the cushion-plant community on the exposed high ridges of Central Otago, New Zealand.

Microclimates

The more severe the climate in which a plant grows, the more important its microclimate is likely to be to its survival and reproduction. Thus the distribution of alpine plants is often strongly influenced by microclimates. Shelter from wind, which chills and desiccates plant tissues, is of key significance. This shelter may be provided by an insulating covering of snow (see chapter 5 for more on the importance of snow cover). But many alpines are not restricted to snowbeds, and these unprotected plants often grow in the shelter provided by other vegetation, rocks and features of the terrain that deflect the prevailing wind. In many cases they have evolved a growth habit and/or morphological features that effectively enable them to provide protective 'phyto-microclimates' for their vulnerable growing points, and developing flowers and fruits. The cushion habit is perhaps the best example of this trait, being ideal for both maximizing heat gain and minimizing heat loss. Surface hairs may provide further protection for the vulnerable growing points and developing flowers and fruits by slowing air movement at the tissue surfaces and thus reducing wind chill.

A study in the Medicine Bow Mountains of Wyoming by Jordan and Smith (1995) showed that if the length of the growing season had been defined only in terms of frost-free days, the 1993 growing season for many plants would have been only five days. However, this study also revealed the considerable importance of microclimates in montane environments: the number and frequency of frosts to which plants were *actually* exposed varied widely, depending primarily on microsite sky exposure and meteorological conditions. Plants that were shielded from sky exposure were less subject to night frosts than unsheltered plants. Those *Erigeron peregrinus* plants growing in the shelter of krummholz sub-alpine firs (*Abies lasiocarpa*) experienced frost only 25 per cent as often as the same species growing out in the open. On calm, clear nights there was a steep vertical temperature zonation within the open alpine meadow, with temperatures coldest near the ground (unless shaded by vegetation). Consequently, flowers borne only 8 cm (3 inches) above the ground were significantly warmer, by some 2°C (3.6°F), than the ground-hugging leaves. When the wind begins to blow, this zonation breaks down and wind-chill exerts an effect. Even so, near the ground, and especially if there is dense vegetation, wind speeds may be substantially reduced by the surface vegetation's roughness, thus diminishing the wind-chill effect.

The 'phyto-microclimates' described above are influenced by the density of the plant, and by leaf shape, size, colour and pubescence. In a study of cushions of *Diapensia lapponica* in Swedish Lapland, it was shown (Fischer and Kuhn 1984) that under summer conditions, with almost continual daylight but much reduced light intensity at night, the outer layers of the cushion warmed up considerably more than the air in the day, causing a steep temperature gradient toward the centre of the cushion. At night these outer layers cooled off more than the air between them as they slowly transferred their heat inwards toward the centre of the cushion and outwards to the air. The diurnal temperature fluctuations in the surface layers of the cushions considerably exceeded those in the soil, but further into the cushion the temperatures remained much more stable. This temperature stability, and the cushion's ability to retain heat gained in the day – which would be lost by a plant with a more open growth habit – is probably important in allowing cushion plants to withstand severe cold, and thus survive in very exposed situations. As such, it is a good example of a freezing avoidance mechanism. Leaf roughness and pubescence are also important factors in determining phyto-microclimates. Wind speed over the leaf surface, and the associated wind chill effect, may be much reduced where the leaf is rough or hairy (**Plate 4.3**), just as rough, woolly outer garments can protect smooth human skin.

Above: 4.3 Densely hairy foliage limits both chilling of leaf surfaces and water loss. *Chaetanthera villosa* growing in a scree, Chilean Andes.

The vulnerability of many high alpines to winter cold in cultivation, particularly when a cold snap comes suddenly after a mild autumn, is at first sight surprising. However, this does not necessarily indicate, as is often supposed, that the species is not hardy; it is more likely that the plants had not received a necessary hardening period before being frozen. In the mountains the hardening process is guaranteed, since the temperature drops rapidly in autumn. This was dramatically illustrated in a study of frost tolerance in *Diapensia lapponica*, which is a drought-tolerant evergreen arctic-alpine cushion plant (Junnila 1985). This study showed that in September, in the wild, the plant was only hardy down to –5°C (23°F), but that frost tolerance increased rapidly during October and remained high until March when the maximum frost resistance was –58°C (–72°F). Subsequently, de-hardening took place and by the beginning of May the maximum frost resistance was back to only –9°C (16°F). The period of winter hardiness was associated with increased tolerance of water deficiency stress, indicating that this species – like many other alpines – can survive with very little water in winter, provided that it is fully dormant at the time.

The most dramatic diurnal montane temperature fluctuations occur in high equatorial mountains where 'summer' comes each day and 'winter' each night (**Plate 4.4**), there being no true seasons but only, in some cases, drier and wetter periods. Plants have adapted to the huge differences between day and night temperatures, often with concomitant daily freeze-thaw cycles, by evolving mechanisms that protect their cells, and particularly their vulnerable growing points, from damage. These mechanisms are similar to those found in arctic-alpines; they include various combinations of physical features (such as thick cell cuticles, hairiness or growing points protected by enfolding foliage) and also biochemical systems within the cells that prevent the cell contents from freezing. It has been shown that some species are able to protect their cells from freezing damage by converting starch, formed during the warm part of the day, into high concentrations of sucrose as night approaches. While starch is insoluble and thus does not affect the freezing point of the cell sap, sucrose is soluble and lowers the freezing point; this allows super-cooling and so protects cells from rupture. (See Beck (1994) for a review of cold-tolerance mechanisms in tropical alpines).

Above: 4.4 Frozen roots in the midday sun. Andes.

Frost tolerance

Alpine plants, with the exception of those that grow only in places with reliable snow cover (such as *Soldanella alpine*), have to be able to survive prolonged periods of sub-zero air temperatures in winter. However, they may have very little tolerance of frost during the growing season, undergoing hardening only as the temperature drops rapidly in autumn. The degree of hardening can be very considerable, *Diapensia lapponica* being hardy only to –5°C (23°F) in the wild in September, but to –58°C (–72°F) at the end of the winter. In cultivation, alpine plants do not experience this rapid drop in air temperatures followed by severe cold that is necessary to stimulate the chemical changes in the cells that confer extreme frost resistance. Accordingly, they may be sensitive to cold that is much less severe than they can generally tolerate in the wild. This explains the otherwise baffling cold damage sometimes exhibited by high alpines in the garden, in particular when a sudden cold spell follows a long, mild autumn. But once plants are frost hardened, they can generally withstand considerable cold and drought.

Tropical mountain plants have to contend with diurnal freeze-thaw cycles as air temperatures rocket during the day and then plummet at night. They achieve this by a range of mechanisms that protect the sensitive growing point at night, so enabling growth processes to resume unaffected each morning.

Once research confirmed that plants from the highest elevations in temperate mountains need to receive a hardening period and then remain dormant throughout the winter if they are to grow successfully, attempts were made to mimic such conditions in cultivation. The well-known developments along these lines at Kew, which included the provision of refrigerated plunge beds in the alpine house, have been described in various articles (for example, Halliwell 1981) and there is no doubt that success has been achieved there with some difficult species. But it is very difficult to mimic natural conditions precisely, and to provide simultaneously for the varied requirements of different species, especially if the reasons for particular conditions are not fully understood. Furthermore, the cost of providing special facilities means that few amateur gardeners are ever likely to consider installing them. Therefore, to reiterate, the best general advice when growing high alpines in pots, troughs or other containers is to ensure, as winter approaches, that the soil is full of roots and also to keep the plants as cool as possible (but not frozen), and the soil only as moist as is necessary to keep the plants turgid.

Plants that predominate on cliffs, windswept ridges and open slopes, where insulating snow cover is absent in winter, have generally evolved effective freezing avoidance or tolerance mechanisms. Measurements in *Loiseleuria procumbens* have shown that diurnal temperature fluctuations in this ground-hugging dwarf shrub, which usually grows on exposed ridges and outcrops devoid of snow cover, to be similar in type – if less in degree – to those of *Diapensia lapponica* (as referred to above). While the influences of snow cover and wind exposure are both very important in determining microhabitats for alpine plants, another profound influence is the aspect of the ground on which the plants are growing. Moser *et al.* (1977) confirmed this fact in a study of leaf surface temperatures of *Ranunculus glacialis*, growing near the upper limit of plant life at 3,184 metres (10,450 feet) altitude in the European Alps. All the plants were growing at the same altitude, but some were growing on a north-facing slope, some on a south-facing slope and some on the ridge between them; the horizontal distance between the plants on the north and south slopes was only c.12 metres (40 feet). Leaf surface temperatures during the growing seasons from 1968-1972 varied between absolute extremes of –12°C and 44°C (10°F and 111°F). Plants growing on south slopes and ridges experienced 60 per cent more hours of above-zero temperatures than the north slope plants. These, in turn, experienced 75 per cent more hours in the range –5-0°C (23-32°F) than the south slope and ridge plants. While about 3 per cent of all hours on the ridge and south slope fell in the 15-30°C (59-86°F) range, such temperatures never occurred on the north slope site. The temperature of –6°C

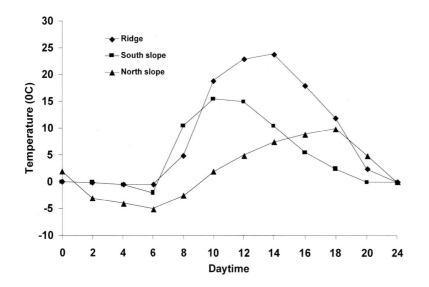

Fig. 4.1
Leaf temperatures of *Ranunculus glacialis* at microhabitats differing in slope direction during a clear day (after Moser *et al.*, 1977).

(21°F), which is critical for freezing damage in summer-active leaves, was measured repeatedly on the north slope and on the ridge (as radiation freezing) but never occurred on the south-facing slope. The data from this study, for one cloud-free day in July 1968, are illustrated in **Figure 4.1**, and show clearly the thermal deficit on the north slope.

The roots of arctic-alpine plants are less in need of special adaptations to withstand severe cold or alternating freeze-thaw than their aerial parts because the mass of the soil exerts a substantial moderating effect on temperature. The chief requirement of plant roots is to be able to withstand long periods of cold or freezing temperatures, rather than the short-term extremes to which the above-ground parts are exposed. Soil and near-ground air temperatures are generally lower during the growing season in arctic than in alpine environments. Because of the lack of solar energy in the long, dark polar winter, the soil freezes, often to a considerable depth, and below the surface layers it never thaws – hence the term 'permafrost' to describe this permanently frozen lower soil. During each growing season a variable, but generally shallow, layer of surface soil eventually thaws out in response to the large amount of solar radiation the surface receives during the long polar summer. So it is that the soil around the roots of *Ranunculus glacialis* in the Arctic is actually below freezing point for nine months of the year. Soil in surface depressions may be constantly waterlogged in summer due to the impermeability of the permafrost below; in consequence, bogs are the prevailing vegetation types in these places. By contrast, once the ice has melted from the surface layers of soil on raised or sloping ground, the lack of summer precipitation (due to the continuous high-pressure system that holds sway over polar weather), along with a general tendency for freely draining soil types, results in rapid drying. The plants that grow in these areas, which include the bulk of the arctic-alpine species, must be drought tolerant – as well as being able to withstand severe cold.

While plants growing on mountains do not normally have to cope with permafrost or severe summer drought, they must be able to withstand the generally greater wind-chill at high elevation (resulting from higher mean and maximum wind speeds). The highest wind speeds are those found in mountains in the southern hemisphere in the zone of the 'Roaring Forties' (the latitudes between 40°S and 50°S), and it is no coincidence that these mountains have the highest proportion of wind-resistant cushion plants among their flora of any in the world. The reduction of biomass production caused by high wind speeds in the mountains seems to be broadly similar to that due to permafrost and summer drought in the Arctic. So, on balance, productivity in arctic and alpine environments is generally similar. And it is also interesting to note that productivity in these cold 'desert' environments is broadly similar to that in hot deserts. In the case of arctic and alpine tundra, lack of energy is the main factor that limits plant growth, while in hot deserts, growth is limited by the lack of a regular supply of water. However, alpine plants can also suffer from drought, particularly in winter and especially if they are growing in open situations, where they are unprotected from the desiccating, icy blast. Though there may be plenty of water around, it may be frozen, and so not available for uptake by plant roots. This situation is known as physiological drought. In addition to having a tolerance for physiological drought, tropical alpine plants often need to withstand actual drought, since many tropical mountain ranges (as examples, parts of the Andes and the Kenyan mountains) have a dry climate, either during the growing season or in some cases all year round.

Tree Lines and Temperature

The commonest definition of an alpine is a plant occurring above the tree line. While as gardeners we often describe many other plants loosely as 'alpines', the definition based on tree lines is a good one from the ecological point of view, since plants growing below the tree line often occur in a range of non-alpine habitats, whereas those from above the tree line generally do not. There is no doubt, also, that tree lines effectively delimit alpine environments, because the effect of a forest on microclimate is so great as to make it quite different from open meadow or tundra (Billings and Mooney 1968). But what determines the position of tree lines, and why are they so abrupt? And how do alpine plants manage to grow where trees cannot? At present we do not have generally agreed-upon answers to these questions; various factors are proposed as being important at different times and by different researchers. The main hypotheses can be put forward briefly as follows:

1. The stress hypothesis: tree growth is impaired by repeated damage caused by freezing, frost desiccation or phototoxic effects after frost.
2. The disturbance hypothesis: mechanical damage caused by wind, ice blasting, snow break and avalanches, or by herbivory and fungal pathogens (these being often associated with snow cover) may remove biomass or meristems to, or above, the amount that can be replaced by growth and development, below certain temperatures.
3. The reproduction hypothesis: pollination, seed development, seed dispersal, germination and seedling establishment may be limited and thus prevent tree recruitment at higher altitudes.
4. The carbon balance hypothesis: either carbon uptake by photosynthesis or the balance between uptake and loss are insufficient to support maintenance and minimum growth of trees.
5. The growth limitation hypothesis: low temperatures limit synthetic processes that lead from the basic building blocks of life, sugars and amino acids, to the complex plant body so that the minimum rates required for growth and tissue renewal are not achieved, regardless of the supply of raw materials by photosynthesis.

Whatever the basic mechanism that precludes tree survival above a certain altitude, it cannot be associated with seasonality because tree lines are formed in non-seasonal climates in the tropics as well as in areas with contrasting summers and winters. It should also be noted that tree lines may establish in maritime areas with negligible frost risk and in the complete absence of ice blasting or snow damage. The most logical conclusion is that different factors have different relative importance, which is dependent on differing situations. For example, in higher latitudes where day length reduces rapidly in autumn and increases rapidly in spring, critical situations may occur during rapid freezing periods if the shoots have not become sufficiently hardened in autumn, or have begun to lose their frost resistance in spring. Similar rapid freezing might have no deleterious effect in midwinter when the shoots are fully hardened. In the tropics, on the other hand, freezing damage could theoretically occur during clear nights at any time of the year, but in practice it seems that frost damage probably rarely plays a decisive role in tropical tree line formation.

Winter desiccation of tree foliage, due to loss of water that cannot be replaced since the soil is frozen, may sometimes be a major cause of tree-line formation. For example, Tranquillini (1979) suggests that winter desiccation sets the krummholz limit in the Alps. Mechanical damage may be important in determining tree lines in areas with high snowfall, frequent avalanches and high wind speeds, but it is unlikely to be of widespread importance. Neither does reproductive capability seem to be a key factor, since scattered tree seedlings are often found well above the tree line. Also, if reproductive limitation is important, then how can krummholz be explained? Similarly, there is little good evidence to support carbon limitation as being of overriding general importance for reasons outlined below. In general, maintaining woody stems, while costly in energy and carbon requirement, does not appear critical to the carbon balance at tree-line altitudes, although as the tree gets bigger the proportion of non-photosynthetic stem tissues increases, adding to the burden.

Körner (1999) has put forward a new growth-limitation hypothesis to explain low temperatures as a causal factor in the creation of tree lines. He expresses his hypothesis through a simple analogy, saying that if one considers a growing tree in the same way as a house under construction, the limitation of growth at tree line is not due to any lack of availability of bricks and mortar (that is the raw materials required for growth), but rather because the bricklayers (the enzymes) are not prepared to work when conditions are too cold! And, because of this, building materials (photosynthates) accumulate to the extent that suppliers (in the tree's case, chiefly photosynthesis) have to slow down or stop deliveries altogether. Then the whole process of 'house building' comes to a halt. In support of his hypothesis, Körner quotes evidence that shoot apical meristems (see Glossary) of trees are colder for most of the growing season than those of ground-hugging alpine plants. The latter benefit from 'body' warming and heat retention in the day (as described above for *Diapensia lapponica*), and from radiative warming by the soil at night. Hence, use of raw materials for growth by the tree meristems is less efficient. This disadvantage is compounded by the fact that tree canopies severely reduce the soil's exposure to solar radiation, so reducing soil temperature. This in turn inhibits root growth, and water and nutrient uptake. Körner quotes research by Munn *et al.* (1978) in Montana, which showed that at 2,300 metres (7,545 feet) elevation, soil temperatures at 50 cm (20 in) below the soil surface were nearly 5°C (41°F) lower under forest, compared with adjacent grassland during the summer. He concludes that limitation of tree root growth, rather than limitation of photosynthesis, is the main reason for the abrupt tree line that often occurs across gradients of only 100-300 metres (330-980 feet) in altitude. Solar radiation does not significantly change over such gradients, at least in the temperate zone, nor does the 1-2°C (34-36°F) mean air temperature difference cause a significant change in photosynthesis. But various studies have shown that no new roots are formed at soil temperatures below

3-5°C (37-41°F), a temperature range commonly found in the growing season among tree roots at the tree line in different montane regions of the world. Studies have also shown that, at these low soil temperatures tree shoot activity, including photosynthesis, is tightly controlled by root activity.

So it seems likely that alpines are able to grow above the tree line because their lower stature, and generally more compact morphology, results in warmer tissue temperatures than those in trees at the same ambient air temperature.

Tree lines

Understanding the significance of tree lines is important when discussing alpine plant ecology because there are fundamental climate differences between woodland and the unwooded mountain slopes above. Hence, the commonly used definition of alpine plants as those that grow above the tree line is valid. There is still considerable disagreement among ecologists over what determines the position of tree lines, why they are generally so abrupt, and how alpine plants are able to grow where trees cannot. This disagreement stems from the fact that the occurrence and position of tree lines seems to be controlled by a range of interacting factors (mean annual temperature, minimum temperature, length of growing season, grazing, disease, physical damage by wind, snow etc., fire, reduced tree growth and breeding success – or due to a combination of these factors). The relative importance of these varies in space and time. It appears that the lower stature and generally more compact morphology of alpine plants bring warmer tissue temperatures than those in trees at the same ambient air temperature. This allows alpines to grow above the tree line.

The elevations of the natural tree line and of the limits to vegetation growth in all the main mountain ranges of the world, from Pole to Pole, are shown in **Figure 4.2**. As common sense would suggest, these limits run more or less parallel to each other, regardless of latitude, and increase in elevation from the Poles toward the

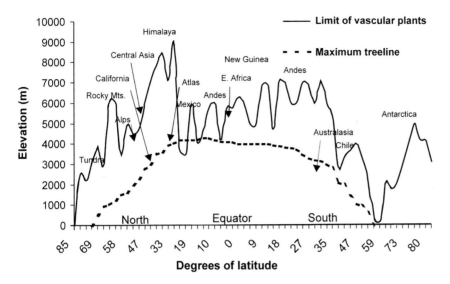

Figure 4.2
Treeline and limits to
alpine vegetation from
Pole to Pole.

equator. Thus the average tree line elevation is only c.1-2,000 metres (3,300-6,600 feet) in the southern Andes of Chile and in Alaska, but rises to 4,000 metres (13,100 feet) in the equatorial mountains of East Africa, Asia and South America.

Two factors that need to be taken into account when explaining puzzling variations in tree line elevation are wind exposure and the influence of human activity. Severe wind exposure can substantially reduce the elevation of the tree line through direct physical impact as well as by lowering air temperatures through wind chill. Also, in many places the natural tree line has been eliminated or fragmented by man, as in substantial parts of continental Europe, North America, the Himalayas, the Andes and Papua New Guinea. In other places the forest has probably always been patchy or absent due to low rainfall, as on the western slopes of the Peruvian Andes and the north slope of Mount Kenya (Smith 1994). Fire has often been purposely used to increase and maintain the amount of grazing land above the forest, particularly in equatorial mountains (Deshmukh 1986), but also in temperate regions. In all these cases, alpine species merge gradually with species of montane pasture, savannah or desert.

It should also be noted that forest patches beyond what is the current 'normal' tree line occur not infrequently in all parts of the world. For instance, in the Swiss Alps near Zermatt groups of *Pinus cembra* occur on rocky outcrops as high as 2,500 metres (8,200 feet), 200-300 metres (660-980 feet) above the general tree line (Körner 1999). Similarly Holtmeier and Broll (1992) describe 'tree islands' c. 400 metres (1,300 feet) above the tree line, in the Rocky Mountains. But this is by no means a record for isolated tree patches: in Venezuela, *Polylepis sericea* stands are found up to 4,200 metres (13,800 feet), i.e. 900 metres (3,000 feet) above the official tree line (Goldstein et al. 1994) and form impressive forests at 4,100 metres

(13,500 feet). Two principal theories have been advanced to explain these apparent anomalies. The first ('shelter') hypothesis suggests that the outpost trees occur in particularly favoured positions (for example in the lee of cliffs or rocks, or among rocks where seedlings are protected from herbivores) and that, once established, they provide each other with mutual shelter. The second ('fossil') hypothesis proposes that these tree islands are remnants of a higher elevation forest, originally established during a warmer climatic period, that have survived at an elevation that is currently too cold for tree establishment. But it is generally impossible to be sure which hypothesis – if either – is correct in any one instance.

Precipitation

Precipitation in mountains generally increases with altitude, because when wind blows against mountains the air rises and is cooled. The water vapour in the cool air subsequently condenses and clouds form. Some mountain peaks are covered by cloud at all times, in particular those close to the sea, from which moist air is blown by a prevailing onshore wind (**Figure 4.3**). And, because of the rising air currents, the windward side of a mountain usually gets more rain or snow than the leeward side. As the air flows over the tops of the mountains and down the other side, it

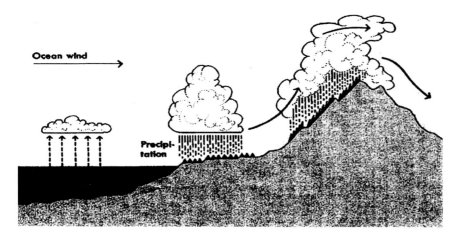

How Geographical Features Affect the Weather

Ocean wind

Precipi-
tation

Figure 4.3
Influence of oceanicity
and topography on
precipitation.

becomes warmer and the clouds evaporate; this is the so-called 'rain shadow effect'. In some mountain ranges the rain shadow effect is very marked, resulting in huge differences in precipitation between the slopes facing towards and away from the prevailing wind, and/or the sun. Thus the south-facing slopes of the central and eastern Himalayas receive considerable monsoon precipitation, while the high Tibetan plateau to the north is very dry. In the Pyrenees the north-facing slopes – especially those at the west end of the range, near the Atlantic – are wet and cool in summer while the southern slopes – particularly at the Mediterranean end – are hot and dry. In the Rocky Mountains a warm dry wind called a Chinook sometimes flows down the eastern slopes. A Chinook may raise the temperature at the foot of the mountains as much as 22°C (70°F) in a few hours, and can melt snow on the ground at the rate of about 2.5 cm (one inch) an hour. Such winds also blow in the Alps and other European mountain systems, where they are known by their German name, Foehns.

The phenomenon of increasing cloudiness with elevation in mountains does not only lead to higher rainfall, it also affects the amount of solar radiation reaching the ground, and hence the temperature. Cloudy mountains are cooler as well as wetter, and are also snowier than mountains in drier, inland regions.

The moisture regime varies considerably between arctic and alpine environments. Precipitation is less in the high Arctic than in the Alps, but permafrost prevents downward movement of water on relatively flat ground in the Arctic, so that in summer the surface soil is usually saturated. However, the prevention of soil leaching by the impermeable permafrost causes accumulation of mineral salts on, or below, the soil surface in amounts that may be sufficient to restrict growth of all except salt-tolerant plants. Paradoxically, the drought involved is similar physiologically to that imposed by salination in hot deserts, although the mechanism is, of course, quite different. In hot deserts, soil salination is caused by evapo-transpiration exceeding precipitation. Either way, all except specially adapted plants are unable to take up water from the saline solution, due to osmotic problems. Saline deserts are actually rare in montane situations because snowmelt and summer rainfall are generally greater than in hot desert regions, so there is more dilution of any salts released from the soil. Where there is mountain permafrost the generally steeper terrain means that water moves over it in summer, travelling through the thawed surface soil. However, there are examples of cold desert with saline soils in dry mountain ranges as, for example, the eastern slopes of the high Andes in Argentina. Plants from areas prone to soil salination are likely to be able to grow satisfactorily in cultivation without the need for added salt: they are adapted to tolerate salt, rather than needing it for their metabolism.

Humid climates, in which precipitation exceeds water demand throughout the growing season (**Plate 4.5**), are much more common in mountainous regions than arid climates, which have, by implication, water shortages at certain times of the year (**Plate 4.6**). Mountainous regions having generally humid summer climates include the Alps, most of Scandinavia, the Caucasus east to Dagestan, the Urals, many mountain areas of southern Siberia, coastally influenced Alaska, the Aleutians, the mountains of Japan, the New Zealand Alps and southernmost South America. In illustration, an annual precipitation profile for the Stelvio Pass, in Italy (**Figure 4.4**), shows plenty of excess water available for plants throughout

Above left: 4.5 Predominantly wet mountains. Shipton La, Nepal.

Above right: 4.6 Summer-dry mountains. Mt Evans, Colorado.

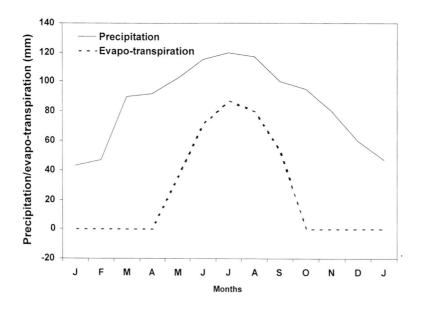

Figure 4.4 Annual precipitation profile for the Stelvio Pass, Italy.

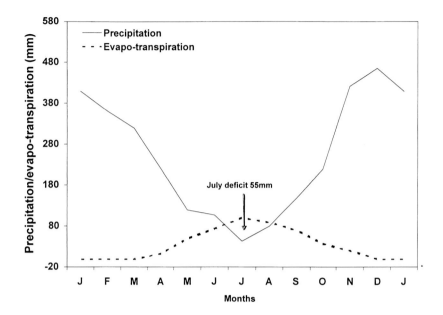

Figure 4.5
Annual precipitation
profile for Mt Rainier,
Cascades, USA.

the growing season, even though the mean annual precipitation is only 782 millimeters (31 inches). Contrast this with the profile for a weather station at the moderate elevation of 1,700 meters (5,600 feet) on Mt Rainier in the Cascades of the State of Washington (**Figure 4.5**): here, plants are likely to suffer drought in July of each year despite a mean annual precipitation of 2,963 millimeters (118 inches) – nearly four times as much as the Stelvio Pass receives. This is because most of the precipitation in the Cascades comes as snow and only about 43 millimeters (1.7 inches) – whether as rain or snow – falls in July. This is 55 millimeters (2 inches) short of potential evapo-transpiration in that month, leading to arid conditions. Other mountain areas with slight to severe summer drought include southern Spain, the eastern Mediterranean, Transcaucasia, Central Asia, continental valleys of Scandinavia, southern Atlas, parts of the Andes and the central and southern Rocky Mountains.

In mountains that are very wet during the growing season there are few, if any, dry places; everything becomes soaked by the omnipresent water and high air humidity. Predictably, therefore, in wet mountains there are few, if any, drought-tolerant (xerophytic) plant species. Some plants, such as *Ranunculus glacialis* and the Himalayan cremanthodiums, are able to grow and flower in soil that is continuously waterlogged during the growing season, and are able to withstand prolonged periods of complete inundation provided the water is not stagnant.

Precipitation in alpine environments

Precipitation generally increases with elevation because rising air cools and, as it does, so the amount of water vapour that it can hold is reduced. As the air, now denuded of much of its water vapour, flows down the leeward slopes of the mountains it warms up, enabling it to hold more water vapour; this process leads to the 'rain shadow effect', in which rain falls on the windward side of a mountain, leaving the leeward side dry. This effect can lead to very marked variations in climate, and associated plant habitats and species, between the slopes of mountains facing or in the lee of prevailing winds. This is particularly the case where prevailing winds come from a nearby sea that is warm enough for the air to pick up and hold abundant moisture as it passes over the surface.

In mountainous areas with predominantly wet growing seasons there are very few dry places; everything becomes soaked by the omnipresent water and high air humidity. As a result these areas yield few, if any, xerophytes. However, in mountains with dry growing seasons there are always some microhabitats where water can reliably be found, often as snowmelt water, and can provide a viable habitat for mesophytic and, in some cases, even hydrophytic vegetation.

In the case of dry mountains, one might think the reverse would be true, and that only xerophytic plants would grow. However, in all but the most extremely arid of the drier mountains, some water accumulates, often as winter snow that becomes available as snowmelt in summer. Where the snowmelt reaches, microsites form, and may have a reliably humid or even wet climate suitable for plants that could not grow in these mountains otherwise. Such mesophytic plants often give away their need for damp habitats by luxuriant foliage, marking them out from the drought-tolerant species that form the majority of the vegetation. A good example is *Primula parryi*, which grows in snowmelt patches and along the stream sides in summer-dry areas of the Rockies (**Plate 4.7**). Compare this plant with its close relatives, *Primula angustifolia* and *P. cusickiana* (**Plate 4.8**), that grow in much drier areas in the same mountains but have xerophytic physiology and morphology (compact growth; smaller stalkless leaves with thicker cuticles and short-stalked flowers). *P. cusickiana* takes adaptation to drought one stage further,

dying down soon after flowering and remaining dormant throughout the hot, dry summer and the long cold winter. This response, known as aestivation, is the standard method for avoiding heat and drought of most bulbous plants. These plants form an especially prominent component of the flora in areas with hot, dry summers, such as the eastern Mediterranean, Middle East, South Africa and California (**Plate 4.9**).

The ease or difficulty of growing plants from extreme environments in our gardens depends on how similar our home climate is, or can be made by artificial means, to these habitats. Thus, on the mild, moist, Atlantic seaboard of Europe and in the north-west of North America, *Primula parryi* is relatively easy to grow outside without protection whereas *P. angustifolia* is much more difficult, with or without protection from excessive summer and winter wet, and *P. cusickiana* is almost impossible. But the reverse might be true in areas with hot, dry summers and cold winters with abundant snow cover.

A unique physiological adaptation has been evolved by one family of flowering plants of interest to alpine gardeners, the Crassulaceae, enabling them to cope with extremely dry environments. Members of this family, which include among others the genera *Cotyledon*, *Jovibarba*, *Sedum* and *Sempervivum*, have evolved an alternative to normal photosynthesis. In most plants, the stomata open during the day and close at night; in the Crassulaceae the stomata stay closed during the day, when water loss would be greatest, and then open up at night. Carbon dioxide for photosynthesis taken up at night is stored in the cells as malic acid and isocitric acid, subsequently used during the day as a carbon source for 'normal' photosynthesis when sunlight is available.

Above left: 4.7 *Primula parryi* is a leafy plant that requires constant moisture during its growing season.

Above right: 4.8 *Primula cusickiana*, with its thick fleshy leaves, is able to tolerate very dry conditions, dying back to a dormant rootstock during the heat of summer.

Above: 4.9 *Fritillaria imperialis*, like many bulbs from regions with Mediterranean climates, remains underground (aestivates) during the long, hot dry summer sun. Zagros Mts, Iran.

The arctic-alpine plants best able to withstand drought (and temperature extremes) are those that occur on the ridges, rocks and open slopes that are not covered by snow in winter and that do not receive snowmelt in summer. Patagonia provides the extreme example of such habitats, as it is one of the windiest places on earth. It is no coincidence that it also has the greatest proportion of cushion plants in its flora, 40 per cent, compared with (for example) 2 per cent in the Rockies. In such windy habitats, soil moisture status is likely to fluctuate wildly during the growing season while, in winter, soil moisture may be locked up in ice. The latter prevents plants from taking up moisture from the soil in order to replace that lost through the evaporative action of wind and sun; in consequence, water stress becomes more severe as the winter goes on. Plants that have adapted to these windswept ridges and rock crevices have low transpiration rates throughout the year. They are, as noted above, often cushions, which may be hairy or have leaves with thick cuticles, both of which limit water loss. In some genera, for example the benthamiellas of the southern Andes, some species have hairy cushions (as in *B. lanata*) while others (for example, *B. longifolia*), see **Plate 4.10**, are hairless. Hairy cushions that are adapted to catch and hold the mist and rain of summer in the mountains are particularly unsuited to the frequent rainfall and high air humidity that they may have to withstand for most of the year in many gardens. This often makes them especially difficult to cultivate without overhead protection in winter.

Below: 4.10 *Benthamiella longifolia*. Estancia Huyuche, Argentina.

Irradiation

Alpine gardeners often consider the difference between the quantity and quality of the light that alpine plants receive at high altitudes in the wild compared to that that they receive at low elevation in our gardens as a major factor in limiting their success with some of the more difficult species. It is often assumed that light intensities are higher in the mountains and that the light is richer in some parts of the spectrum, notably the ultra-violet (UV), and that this results in more compact growth and more, better-coloured flowers. Research has shown that light intensity does indeed generally intensify with increasing altitude because of the reduction of dust and particulate pollutants in the atmosphere. The amount of light energy received will depend upon day length during the growing season, as well as light intensity. Day length in summer increases with latitude, so plants growing farther north or south receive greater light exposure during their short growing season than plants growing in equally hostile conditions (at higher elevations), but nearer the equator. However, since plants growing near the equator experience almost uniform day length throughout the year, they are able to continue growing, and so accumulate as much, or more, energy as their alpine counterparts. Light intensity at ground level is very much affected by how much cloud is present: plants growing on mountains in the temperate zone, with clear summer skies, receive more light energy than those where summer rainfall is high. Also, not all alpines grow in open situations, some being restricted to caves and shady rock crevices where they receive much less light, and at a lower intensity. Examples are the ramondas (**Plate 4.11**) and haberlaeas, the widespread little yellow violet of the European mountains (*Viola biflora*) and Farrer's 'Ancient King', *Saxifraga florulenta*, which grows on the shady faces of granite cliffs in the Maritime Alps.

The situation regarding UV is more complicated, and even more affected by how much cloud is present. The UV-B (the portion of UV that affects plants most) received at ground level is a combination of the direct ('beam') UV coming straight from the sun, and that reflected back from the sky. While beam UV does increase with altitude, sky UV often decreases, especially in cloudy mountains. The net result is generally a slight increase in total UV-B with elevation in mountains that generally have little cloud cover in summer (Caldwell 1968). There is also a latitudinal

Below: 4.11 *Ramonda myconi* generally grows in shady crevices or in moist woodland where it escapes the hottest midday sun. Odessa Canyon, Pyrenees.

influence, with UV-B irradiation being greatest at the tropics and declining towards the poles. Therefore, tropical mountains receive the highest natural levels of UV-B found anywhere in the world. The mean daily UV-B irradiance received at tropical, high-elevation sites (corrected for day length) can be nearly six times that of the maximum dose received at arctic latitudes (Caldwell *et al.*, 1980).

Light intensity and UV

Light intensity generally increases with increasing altitude because of the reduction of dust and particulate pollutants in the atmosphere. However, the amount of light received by alpine plants will also vary depending upon latitude and how much cloud is present. In the temperate zone, day length during the growing season increases with latitude, while plants growing on mountains with clear summer skies will receive more light energy than those inhabiting mountains with high summer rainfall.

The amount of UV in the light received by alpines varies considerably dependent, primarily, on the amount of cloud cover. Generally there is a slight increase in UV-B (the most important fraction of UV with regard to plant growth) with altitude, provided skies are clear, but no change or even a decrease when clouds obscure the sun. UV-B irradiation also decreases with increasing latitude, so tropical mountains receive the most. The slight differences in UV found in mountains in the temperate zone appear to have little influence on plant growth or development, including flower production.

An interesting study compared the responsiveness to UV-B of species grown from seed that were collected from a number of locations along a 3,000-metre (9,850-feet) elevational gradient in Hawaii. The plants were subjected to different levels of artificial UV-B, simulating levels occurring at the different elevations (Sullivan *et al.* 1992). This experiment revealed that, in general, sensitivity to UV-B decreased with elevation of seedlot. That is, those species that came from the higher elevations, where natural UV-B irradiance is greater, were less sensitive. Of particular interest to the alpine gardener was the finding that, of the 33 species tested, UV-B radiation significantly reduced plant height in 14 species, and

Left: 4.12 *Viola calcarata* (photographed here on Mt Cenis, French Alps), while difficult to grow, remains in character if success is achieved.

biomass in eight species (that is, the plants were more compact), but in the others it had no significant effect. However, in no species was plant height increased following exposure to more UV-B than it would receive in its natural habitat. But this research was done in the most extreme situation, a high, sub-tropical mountain, having UV-B levels far greater than those found in the mountains from which most of our hardy arctic-alpine plants originate.

A more relevant study was done at a 3,500-metre (11,500-feet) field study site in Colorado, in which UV filters were suspended above the vegetation. Removal of UV-B had very little effect on plant growth or flowering. In one species of clover, removal of UV increased rather than decreased flowering, but there were no significant effects in five other species (Caldwell et al., 1980). Thus it seems that we are probably wrong when we blame low UV-B levels for lax growth and poor flowering of high alpines in our gardens. And if UV were really important for maintaining alpine plants 'in character', and for enhancing flowering, it would not be possible to grow good specimens under glass, since glass screens out most of the UV light. A visit to an AGS Show soon dispels this possibility, since most of the near-perfect specimens of high-alpine species on display are grown permanently under glass. Nevertheless, the fact remains that there are some species (for example, *Androsace alpina*, *Saxifraga stolitzkae* and rosulate violas) that are notoriously difficult to keep in character under glass; it remains a mystery why they seem particularly prone to etiolation while their close relatives (such as *Androsace vandellii*, *Viola calcarata* (**Plate 4.12**) and *Saxifraga georgei* do not. Probably, in most cases where plants grow out of character under glass, this is due to the reduction in light intensity at sea level, particularly in towns, rather than to any lack of UV. This is especially likely in an over-shaded alpine house or frame or one with dirty glass. Other cultural factors, notably overfeeding, may also contribute to etiolation.

5·THE IMPACT OF SNOW COVER

The significance of snow cover to the survival and growth of alpines was touched on in Chapter 3. However, the importance of snow cover is of such crucial importance in determining the distribution and abundance of alpine plant species that it merits a much more detailed discussion. The protective aspects of snow cover are easily listed: protection from low temperature extremes, winter desiccation, ice blast and solar radiation (the latter being potentially dangerous to dormant tissue). The adverse effects of snow cover are less often considered, but are also important. Shortening of the growing season as the result of reduced irradiation is the most obvious and best researched of these. Other less obvious disadvantages of being under snow are likely to include waterlogging, as the snow melts and causes soil and above-ground anoxia; mechanical pressure and shearing effects when snow moves, as often happens on steep slopes; snow mould and other specialist pathogens that have evolved to live in – or under – the snow, and snow rodents that burrow beneath the snow and eat whatever plant material they find. The significance of these beneficial and adverse effects of snow cover depends, to a considerable extent, on both the duration and depth of snow lie. The amount of time plants are covered by snow depends on many variables, where the timing, amount and duration of snowfall, and the length of any intervening periods without snow cover, are all clearly crucial. Some mountain regions have much higher snowfall than others (see the section on precipitation in Chapter 4), and snowfall persists for varying lengths of time, depending on a wide range of factors. These include latitude, elevation, aspect, topography and windiness. In general, snow melts faster on mountains that are nearer the equator, and melts at lower elevations in any particular latitudinal zone. In the northern hemisphere snow persists longer on north-facing slopes than on slopes facing the sun but, given that generalization, topography is also very important. Snow gathers in some places, mainly in dips and around obstructions such as rocks (**Plate 5.1**), and is shed from

Left: 5.1 Undulating terrain with rocks causing variations in accumulation and lie of snow.

others, such as windswept ridges and cliff faces (**Plate 5.2**). Wind blows snow from one place to another, often exposing plants that were covered, and re-covering plants that had previously emerged from primary snow cover. In some cases at high altitudes in areas with high snowfall there may be no snow-free period in some years, and alpines may have to survive one or two years of permanent snowpack. On the other hand, in years when snowfall is light, plants that are usually covered with a protective snow blanket for many months may remain exposed, which may result in severe damage or even death.

Above: 5.2 *Saxifraga spruneri* growing on a steep cliff on Mt Olympus, Greece, which will remain free of snow cover even in winter.

Beneficial and adverse effects of snow cover

Snow cover has a major impact on the survival, growth and reproduction of alpine plants. The benefits of snow cover to alpines include protection from extreme low temperatures, winter desiccation, ice blast and damaging solar radiation during the dormant period. The costs include shortening of the growing season, soil waterlogging during snowmelt, physical pressure and shearing effects when snow moves, snow moulds and the fact that snow also provides cover and protection for rodents and other herbivores. The significance, and balance, of these beneficial and adverse effects of snow cover depends largely on duration and depth of snow lie. Snow that persists has a greater limiting effect on plant growth and reproduction than snow that melts earlier in the season. Deep snow takes longer to melt than shallow snow, but provides the plants with greater insulation from cold air and soil freezing.

In a study of the effects of a snow-free period on the phenology of alpine plants inhabiting snow patches, Kudo (1991) found that contraction of the snow-free period, as occurs in late-lying snow patches, reduced flowering and seeding rates in a wide range of species. Shrubs, especially evergreen species such as *Phyllodoce aleutica* and *Harrimanella stelleriana*, took longer to mature their seeds. In the sites with the shortest snow-free periods they abandoned sexual reproduction altogether and reproduced vegetatively by layering. Non-woody plants opened their flowers, even in the habitats with only short snow-free periods, but fruit-set was reduced in many species, such as *Veronica stelleri* var. *longistyla* and *Solidago virga-aurea* var. *leiocarpa*. *Primula cuneifolia* and *Potentilla matsumurae*, both quick-flowering species that maintained their flower number throughout the snow-melting gradient, were considered the most successful species in the habitats with late-lying snow (Kudo 1992). Some grasses and sedges shifted their leaf habit from summer green to semi-evergreen in response to decreasing periods of release from snow cover; this shift being considered a strategy that enables the plants to extend their period of photosynthetic activity.

A number of studies have shown an approximately linear negative correlation between the thickness of snow cover and the depth of soil freezing (Sakai and Larcher 1987). When alpine soils freeze during the early part of the winter due to lack of snow, later snowfalls can cause soil temperatures to rise again, and soils may even thaw despite decreasing ambient air temperatures. Except for exposed ridges, rock ledges and other extremely wind-exposed terrain, it can be assumed that soils in the lower alpine belt (just above the tree line) of the temperate zone remain unfrozen for most if not all of the year, provided autumn snowfalls are not delayed for too long. At higher elevations and/or higher latitudes, thicker and earlier snow cover is required in order to prevent the soil freezing.

The complete absence of snow during the winter may cause soils to freeze to great depth and expose plants to severe physical and physiological stress. An extreme example is found in parts of the semi-arid sub-tropical Andes in north-west Argentina, where plants of a very rich alpine flora have to survive six months of winter at altitudes of 4,000-5,000 metres (13,100-16,400 feet), mostly bare of snow protection.

The degree of thermal insulation provided by snow was shown in early studies by Eckel and Thams (1939), who found that a snow layer only 35 cm (14 in) thick maintained soil temperatures near zero when ambient air temperatures reached −33°C (−27°F). In a more recent study in one of the coldest areas of the world, in eastern Siberia, a mere 20-cm (8-in) snow layer was found to delay subsoil freezing by two months, during which ambient air temperatures fell to below −40°C

(−40°F) (Zimov *et al.* 1993). While strongly influenced by duration and depth of cover, the insulating property of snow is, in addition, significantly influenced by the type of snow; freshly fallen low-density snow insulates much better than compacted old snow. Hence when fresh fallen snow compacts to become 'old snow', the thermal insulation it provides is reduced by a factor of ten (Körner 1999). The formation of a crust of ice, through freeze-thaw processes, causes thermal insulation to decrease by a further factor of four (Geiger 1965). One should note that the snow that falls in temperate lowland gardens generally becomes compacted more quickly than that falling at higher elevations in the mountains; this is because freeze-thaw is more pronounced in the garden. Because of this, any snow cover that we may get in our gardens is likely to be less useful as an insulator than a similar depth of snow would be in the mountains.

Because it is relatively warm under snow, plants that grow there do not need to be as protected against severe cold as those plants that grow in more exposed situations. This is indicated in **Figure 5.1**, which compares both the above-ground and below-ground freezing resistance of the alpine snowbed species *Soldanella alpina* with that of *Silene acaulis*, a species that commonly grows in snow-free habitats. Numbers indicate summer and winter maximum frost resistance in °C and, in brackets, °F (modified from Larcher 1980). Thus while the difference between the summer and winter cold tolerance of shoots of the snowbell is only 14°C (28°F) that of moss campion is 186°C (306°F).

Figure 5.1
Year-round variation in cold tolerance of above- and below-ground parts of *Soldanella alpina* (snowbed species) and *Silene acaulis* (scree/rock cushion species).

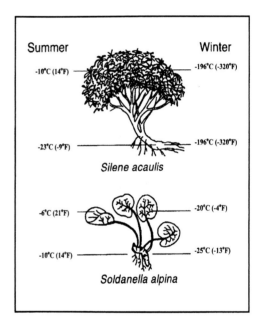

Impacts of snow on plant distributions

By enhancing environmental heterogeneity, snow cover greatly influences patterns of plant distribution. Small changes in microtopography affect the duration and depth of snow lie, and these are reflected in mosaic arrangements of plant species and communities. Plants growing in areas remaining uncovered by snow in winter may be subject to frequent freeze-thaw cycles that do not affect neighbouring plants, growing in nearby snowbeds. So important is the influence of snow that different species have evolved to cope with snow cover of particular depth and duration.

Left top: 5.3 *Loiseleuria procumbens* is able to grow on exposed rocky ridges because it has ground-hugging stems with needle-like leaves that resist water loss, and adventitious roots along the stems that seek out surface water from melting snow.

Left middle: 5.4 Hairy leaf surfaces also serve to conserve moisture in species such as the silver-leaved *Senecio uniflorus* growing in exposed situations. Ostafa, Italian Alps.

Left bottom: 5.5 *Rhododendron ferrugineum* is a typical snowbed shrub having relatively large leaves with thin cuticles ill-equipped to restrict water loss.

Snowbed plants are generally more luxuriant in their growth than plants of open alpine habitats. This is partly because of the protection from winter cold and desiccation that snow cover provides, but also because they have a surer supply of water in the growing season, principally from snowmelt. Thus snowbed plants generally remain green and turgid throughout the growing season. Plants that grow on open sites (as examples, moss campion and dwarf alpine azalea, *Loiseleuria procumbens*), need to be more drought tolerant and are characterized by more compact growth and leaves with thicker cuticles. *L. procumbens* is perfectly adapted to withstand drought, having low transpiration rates as a result of its dense, ground-hugging stature and small, needle-like leaves (**Plate 5.3**). Hairy leaves also conserve water effectively, and many high alpines that grow in exposed environments, including cushion plants such as *Androsace helvetica* and *Eritrichium nanum*, and leafy herbs such as *Senecio uniflorus*, have this adaptation (**Plate 5.4**). *Loiseleuria procumbens* has an additional adaptation to withstand drought: it is able to take up surface meltwater late in the winter through shallow adventitious roots when most of the soil is frozen. In contrast, its ericaceous cousin, the Alpenrose (*Rhododendron ferrugineum*), is intolerant of drought at any time of year, having an open, bushy habit and relatively large leaves with thinner cuticles (**Plate 5.5**). It generally grows in snowbeds that retain snowmelt water in summer. But if the snow melts earlier than usual in spring, or is removed by avalanches, strong winds from an unusual direction or humans (for, or during, skiing), and the plants are exposed to cold, drying winds, they lose water rapidly and may be killed in a few days. As a result it is not uncommon to see severely wind-scorched Alpenrose plants at the edges of snowbanks and in off-piste areas. Similarly, stands of dwarfed coniferous trees can often be found at the tree line, all of which have their upper crowns completely brown and dead above the snow line of the previous winter (**Plate 5.6**).

Left: 5.6 Sub-alpine fir (*Abies lasiocarpa*) 'flag trees' showing browning of leader shoots that will have been repeatedly exposed above the snow in winter. Nihwot Ridge, Colorado.

Another factor that is of critical, but varying, importance to snowbed plants is radiation stress at emergence. Within a few days, or even a few hours when snow melts quickly, emerging plants are exposed to very high intensities of solar radiation, exacerbated by reflection from the remaining snow in their immediate vicinities. The yellow or reddish colour of many freshly emerged snowbed plants results from the lack of green chloroplasts during this phase, which both reduces short wave absorption and allows cells to expand and develop a protective screen, before their photosynthetic 'machinery' is fully installed (Körner 1999). However, some species, notably soldanellas, emerge from beneath snow cover with fully active green leaves – so they have clearly evolved a means of coping with this sudden, high level of insolation.

In addition to the potentially harmful physical and chemical stresses associated with living much of the time under snow there are biological threats, notably from microbial pathogens. Prolonged temperatures close to freezing provide ideal growing conditions for certain fungi that are collectively known as 'snow mould'. Careful examination of plants emerging from snow cover generally reveals infection, and damage tends to be worse for those plants that have been covered the longest. However, herbaceous snowbed plants that overwinter completely below ground, such as North American *Pulsatilla occidentalis*, Australian *Ranunculus anemoneus* and European *Crocus vernus* ssp. *albiflorus*, are able to avoid or minimize damage caused by snow mould.

The importance of snowbeds in determining patterns of plant distribution in alpine vegetation illustrates once again the pronounced influence of microenvironments on plant species and communities. Environmental heterogeneity at particular sites is generally greater in the mountains than in the Arctic tundra because of the greater variability in elevation, slope, aspect, topographic irregularity and soils that, in turn, are reflected in more diverse microclimates and in soil nutrient and water status. The effects of microenvironment may be pronounced, even over distances as small as a few centimetres. For example, small changes in microtopography make a marked difference to soil temperature, depth of thaw, wind effects, snow drifting and resultant protection to leaves, buds and stems. The microtopographic effect may be caused by a rock, a peat hummock or by another plant. Areas remaining uncovered by snow in winter may be subject to frequent freeze-thaw cycles, resulting in frost heave of soil, rocks and plants, while snow-covered areas nearby may be unaffected. This, and the variation in moisture status, results in much local patterning of the vegetation in both Alpine (Schaefer and Messier 1995) and Arctic (Humphries *et al.* 1996) environments. Gibson and Kirkpatrick (1985) showed similar snow cover effects on plant communities even in Tasmania, where climate precludes extensive areas of prolonged snow lie.

The various ways in which individual plant species have evolved to deal with snow cover, some of which have been discussed above, are both interesting and unpredictable, as demonstrated by an ingenious snowbed experiment done in the Rocky Mountains (Galen & Stanton 1995). They first mapped the distribution of snowbed species along a gradient from 80 to 35 days of annual snow-free period, and then manipulated snowpack duration at either end of the gradient by either removing snow early or adding snow when it began to melt. They found that snowbed species fell into at least three categories of microhabitat preference along the snowmelt gradient. *Geum rossii*, *Artemisia scopulorum* and *Sibbaldia procumbens* were more frequently found near the margins of the snowbed, while *Ranunculus adoneus* reached greatest cover halfway to the centre and *Trifolium parryi* was equally abundant everywhere. All five snowbed specialists were able to grow in the centre, but none of them exhibited a 'preference' (in the sense of greatest relative abundance) for this position, which had the shortest growing season at 35 days. The speed of initial growth and development differed among these species. *Ranunculus adoneus* was the first to flower and initiate leaf expansion, and *Trifolium* was the last, the sequence of species flowering being the same at all points sampled. Once growth was initiated, the duration of the vegetative flush was shorter for those species that started late, and longer for those that had started early (*Geum rossii* was in the middle of the range).

Impacts of snow on plant growth and development

Photosynthesis under snow contributes little to the fixation of carbon required for plant growth and development, so plants growing in snowbeds are inhibited until the snow melts. However, snowbed plants are able to compensate for this loss of photosynthetic activity by rapidly increasing their photosynthetic rates once they are released from snow cover. Soil fertility is also less under snow than in the open and least under the deepest and longest-lying snow. However, snow can become an important source of soluble nutrients, providing a boost to the emerging plants once the snow melts.

Galen and Stanton also noted that any annual manipulation of the timing of snowmelt, if carried out over three years or more, had greater cumulative effects on ground cover of the 'fast' starters – those plants that quickly commence growth once the snow melts. The 'fast' starters may benefit from earlier snowmelt through maintaining a greater metabolic preparedness for growth under snow, but this requires greater expenditure of energy in a situation where none can be recouped by photosynthesis. Thus there may be a threshold period under prolonged snow cover when the continued maintenance of a state of metabolic readiness becomes counterproductive; this may be the reason why *Ranunculus adoneus* was found to be less successful in the centre of the snowbed.

Growth and Photosynthesis Under Snow

It is unlikely that photosynthesis under the snow contributes much to the annual fixation of carbon required for plant growth and reproduction. This is not surprising when one realizes that transmittance of solar radiation decreases exponentially with snow depth (**Figure 5.2**). Thus beneath as little as 10 cm (4 in) of snow cover light intensity is only one third of ambient light, falling to zero penetration beneath 30 cm (12 in) of snow. The absence of effective

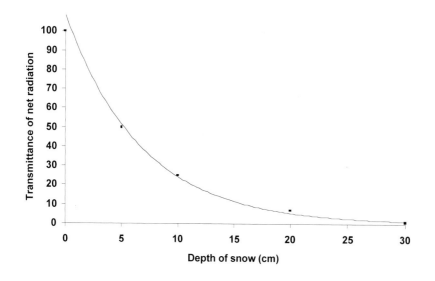

Figure 5.2
Transmittance of sunlight through snow.

photosynthesis under snow was demonstrated in a study of *Erythronium grandiflorum* (**Plate 5.7**) in the central Rocky Mountains by Hamerlynck and Smith (1994) who found that *net* photosynthesis both beneath the snow (allowing for energy lost by respiration) and also on the first day after emergence was negative. However, photosynthetic capacity increased rapidly thereafter and reached a steady positive state by the end of the second day. This suggests that, rather than pre-emergence metabolic activity, it is the rapid 'gearing up' of photosynthesis following emergence that enables this very characteristic snowbed species to cope with a very short growing season. These authors, and Galen and Stanton (1995), also note that snowbed plants growing in smaller snowbeds, which emerge earlier than those in large snowbeds (that linger longer), are always bigger at emergence. This is probably because the plants growing in the smaller snowbeds have a longer growing season each year in which to build up below-ground reserves.

Left: 5.7 *Erythronium grandiflorum* flowers immediately the snow recedes. Olympic Mountains, Washington State, USA.

Soil Fertility Under Snow

Soil fertility, along with availability of solar energy, limits the growth rate of plants that inhabit snowbeds. As a rule, it has been found that early melting zones in snowbeds have richer soils than late melting ones. This is largely because those in early melting zones contain more humus as a result of greater biomass accumulation in previous years. As a general rule, early melting snowbeds also support more plant species than late melting sites, probably also partly as a result of their greater soil fertility (Stanton *et al.* 1994). It is worth noting that snow itself is an important source of soluble nutrients (as well as pollutants, see Chapter 7), which accumulate over the winter and are released rapidly as the snow melts (Bowman 1992). Bilbrough *et al.* (2000) compared nitrogen acquisition by alpine and arctic tundra plants during snowmelt and assessed its significance relative to season-long nitrogen demand. They then related plant responses in both alpine and arctic tundra, to soil and air temperature. All arctic and alpine plants acquired nitrogen during snowmelt. However, alpine plants acquired 100 times more nitrogen than arctic plants. The nitrogen taken up under the snow by alpines equated to 10 per cent of season-long demand, but that taken up by arctic tundra plants only accounted for 0.1 per cent of season-long demand. Soil temperatures were similar in the two systems during snowmelt, averaging –0.4°C (31.3°F) in the arctic and –0.5°C (31.1°F) in the alpine tundra. However, arctic plants experienced lower average winter soil temperatures than alpine plants, at –7.7°C (18.1°F) compared with 2.43°C (36°F), and lower minimum winter soil temperatures, at –14.5°C (6°F) compared with –6.1°C (21°F). Thus, the differences in plant nitrogen uptakes are more likely to be due to winter conditions than conditions during uptake. Either way, plant uptake of nitrogen during snowmelt is important in alpine systems but unimportant in arctic tundra.

6·GEOLOGY AND SOILS

Geology

Understanding rocks, and how they came to be formed, is essential for plant ecologists, and also very helpful for alpine gardeners. Crevices within rock provide anchorage for plants (**Plate 6.1**); fractures and pore spaces both retain water and provide drainage, and rock disintegration provides both the mineral basis of soil and its vital nutrients, and determines soil chemistry. On an altogether larger, world scale, the great mountains that host many of the major alpine environments were built by geological processes, and the evolution of plant and other life on Earth can be interpreted from remains preserved in the rock record.

This chapter introduces the common rocks and the processes that form them, and then goes on to describe the typical landscapes various rocks produce. Finally, the different processes of rock disintegration are described, as the essential precursors to soil development and structure.

Importance of Time

Landslides, earthquakes and volcanic eruptions are reminders that the Earth is not as stable as it might seem from day to day but is dynamic and capable of immense change. Historical archives support this reality, recording that coastlines and river courses have migrated over the last few centuries. However, going even further back in time, the sequence of rocks shows that the Earth's surface has been, and continues to be, reshaped over many years, and contains evidence for ancient seas and continental land masses configured very differently from those we see today. Though some changes are sudden, and others occur within a generation or so, the evidence shows that most take place over a much longer time-scale. Time is therefore a basic concept when understanding how the Earth's surface has arrived at its current form.

Above: 6.1 *Paraquilegia grandiflora* growing in a joint crevice in granite. Barskoon, Tien Shan, Kyrgystan.

Eon	Era	Period		Age (in millions of years)	
Phanerozoic				0	
	Cenozoic	Quaternary			Ice age
				1.8	
		Neogene*	Pliocene		
				5.3	
			Miocene		Uplift of the Himalayas
				24	
		Palaeogene*	Oligocene		
				34	
			Eocene		Spread of grasses
				55	
			Paleocene		
				65	
	Mesozoic	Cretaceous			Rise of angiosperms (flowering plants)
				142	
		Jurassic			Break-up of Pangaea Lycopods and conifers dormant
				205	
		Triassic			
				248	
	Palaeozoic	Permian			Assembly of Pangaea complete Forests of seed plants widespread
				290	
		Carboniferous			
				354	
		Devonian			Caledonian mountains built First vascular land plants
				418	
		Silurian			
				443	
		Ordovician			Explosion of life in the sea
				495	
		Cambrian			
				545	
Proterozoic					
				2500	
Archaean					Earliest life on Earth (c 3500)

* Previously jointly known as the 'Tertiary'.

Table 6.1:
Geological time-scale.

Periods of time involving tens, hundreds or perhaps thousands of years are relatively easy to appreciate. But geological time, measured in millions of years, is so immense as to be barely imaginable to us: to say that the Earth was formed some 4,600 million years ago is beyond our comprehension. An analogy may help in attempting to understand such vast periods of time: if we imagine the entire history of the Earth as a single day, then terrestrial vascular plants became well established by about 9:45 pm, huge forests of gymnosperms by 10:15 pm, and flowering plants (angiosperms) began to emerge by 11:15 pm. Continuing the analogy; the most recent glacial period began less than 2 seconds before midnight (c. 90,000 years ago) and, on this time-scale, mankind has only been around for about 4 seconds (195,000 years). Geological time is divided into the periods shown in **Table 6.1**.

Driving Forces for Change

The modern-day landscape has evolved during a very short period of geological time and represents a snapshot within a constantly evolving system. Setting aside man's efforts in shaping the landscape, three principal energy sources drive these changes. Firstly, radiant solar energy reaching the Earth's surface controls the climate, and thus the major erosive powers of water, wind and ice that shape the surface of the planet. The down-slope flow of the products of erosion is, in turn, influenced by the potential energy of the Earth's gravitational attraction, our second source of energy: gravity also plays a significant part in retaining the atmosphere and hydrosphere close to the Earth, thus enabling the biosphere to develop. The third important energy source is heat produced by radioactive decay within the interior of the Earth; conduction and convection transfer the heat to the surface, resulting in volcanic eruptions and earthquakes. This heat source is also responsible for the long-term, large-scale changes in shape, size and relative positions of the continents during geological time. Evidence for continental drift, the amalgamation of continents into larger masses, and their subsequent break up, has been provided – importantly – by the distribution of fossil plants in the rock record (see also Chapter 9).

Plate Tectonics

Plate tectonics (the movement of the plates that make up the surface of the Earth) are now generally thought responsible for both continental drift and the building of new mountain chains.

The outer solid layer of the Earth, its crust, consists of two components that form the continents and the ocean floors. The continental crust is made up of a great variety of rock types and ranges from those about 3,800 million years in age, in parts of Greenland to the rocks that are in the process of forming today. The continental crust is typically 35-40 km (22-25 miles) thick, but may be more than 90 km (56 miles) beneath the largest mountain chains. By contrast, the ocean crust is composed of mainly basalt, overlain by a thin skin of sediment, and is much thinner, only 7-10 km (4-6 miles).

The crust and the uppermost part of the underlying mantle (the interior zone of the Earth that is directly below the crust, consisting of relatively dense rocks), together make up the lithosphere, which is divided into a number of rigid plates. The boundaries between these plates are zones where most earthquakes and volcanic activity occur. There are three sorts of junction: firstly, constructive zones – where new lithosphere is formed; secondly, destructive zones – where one plate descends back into the Earth's mantle, and is consumed, along what are called subduction zones; and thirdly, transform faults along which plates slide against each other (as, for example, along the San Andreas Fault in California).

New lithosphere is formed along linear volcanic ridges in the middle of the ocean basins. Magma (molten rock) rises up from the mantle as the ocean floor splits apart, and is injected into the parting crust, erupting as basalt on the ocean floor. Each of the major ocean basins is spreading at a very slow rate (the Atlantic ocean, for example, is widening at about the same rate as fingernails grow!) and, as more and more lithosphere is made, the older parts are conveyed further and further away from where they were formed. On reaching the ocean margins, for example around the rim of the Pacific Ocean, the now cold, dense basalt sinks back into the Earth's mantle along subduction zones, in the process generating earthquakes and magma, which is erupted to form volcanoes. The impressive volcanoes of the Andes in South America, for example, lie above one of these subduction zones. In this manner oceanic crust is constantly recycled, and none of the crust present today is older than about 200 million years.

Continental crust is less dense than its oceanic counterpart and will not sink. Thus, when continents collide, the vast piles of sediment deposited along their margins are squeezed intensely; one continent may be driven over another, and this is how huge mountain chains are built. This is what happened, mostly during the Oligocene and Miocene periods (see **Table 6.1**), when an ancient ocean, the Tethys Sea, closed resulting in its sedimentary rock layer being pushed against Europe and Asia, situated to its north, by the northward movement of the African and Indian land masses, situated to its south; the rocks were folded and forced upwards and laterally to form the immense mountain chains of the Alps and Himalayas. The effects of these huge movements in the Alps crumpled some of the younger rocks of southern Britain, for example in Dorset and the Isle of Wight.

Since the first period of collision between these continents, the Himalayas, to provide an example, have been rising at rates of 1-10 millimetres (0.04-0.4 inches) per year, and are one of many parts of the Earth's surface that are rising, while others are sinking. These movements are due to an adjustment process, called isostacy, in which, broadly speaking, the Earth's crust adjusts to 'float' in a higher or lower position, dependent on changes in the weight of the crust. Areas of the Earth's crust will undergo subsequent adjustment as a result of mountain building. Erosion also plays a part: when weight is removed, as in the removal of vast volumes of rock waste during rapid erosion, the isostatic balance is disturbed – in this case the mountains become lighter, so the isostatic adjustment lifts the crust upwards (similar to a boat floating higher in the water if ballast is removed). Thus, the hugely impressive landforms of the Himalayas result from the interplay between the thrusting of India beneath Asia, isostatic uplift and the forces of erosion acting on the rocks. In time, uplift and erosion will reveal deeper and deeper levels within the interior of the mountain belt.

Elsewhere, vertical isostatic movements of the crust are related to the ice age. The glaciated continents of the northern hemisphere were depressed by the immense weight of ice that formed above the crust at the beginning of this period. As the ice melted, some 13,000 years ago in Britain, the surface rebounded again, and rose upwards. Uplift continues today in places such as Scandinavia while, in Antarctica, the crust remains depressed beneath the ice cap.

The Rock Cycle

Around 90 per cent of the Earth's crust is made up from a combination of the elements oxygen, silicon, aluminium and iron. The next most abundant elements are calcium, sodium, potassium and magnesium, and the remaining elements comprise only about 1.5 per cent of the crust. All these elements are combined to form a great variety of minerals, only some of which co-exist to form rocks. Most minerals are stable only in the environment in which they were formed, and will change as they cycle through different conditions. This process of change is described below as the 'rock cycle'.

The continental landscape, in particular the mountains, is under constant attack as a result of erosion by wind, water and ice. Minerals and rock fragments liberated by these powerful forces are carried by rivers and laid down along river beds, in lakes and, ultimately, in the ocean basins. The three great rivers that rise on the Tibetan Plateau, to the north of the Himalayas, carry between them 20 per cent of the sediment dumped annually into the world's ocean basins. The thick piles of silt, sand and gravel that accumulate in the basins are gradually converted to rock as water is squeezed out of the sediment. In time, grains become cemented by newly formed minerals, and the unconsolidated sediment is transformed into rock.

Burial of rocks deep in the Earth's crust, particularly within mountain belts, subjects them to rising temperatures and pressures, such that many of the minerals formed at the surface can no longer exist. The sedimentary rock is thus transformed, or metamorphosed, into rocks such as pelite or psammite, which are composed of minerals that are stable under these new conditions. In some areas, temperature and pressure may be high enough to melt the rocks, producing a liquid that may be injected into other rocks and cools to form a crystalline (igneous) rock. Some of the granites of the high Himalayas have formed in this way.

The formation and recycling of the ocean floor rocks, and the invasion of the crust by magma, has already been described, as part of the widely accepted plate tectonics theory. During these processes some elements are transferred from the inner parts of the planet to the crust. Moreover, many volcanic eruptions emit carbon dioxide and aerosol-forming gases (such as sulphur dioxide) into the atmosphere, with possible consequences for climate change. Significant amounts of carbon dioxide are released into the oceans as a result of rapid erosion of limestone massifs. Conversely, large volumes of atmospheric carbon dioxide are locked up during the formation of limestone, as most notably happened during Cretaceous times with the deposition of the very widespread Chalk rock from billions of tiny calcareous organisms. Thus, the rock cycle is a complex system in which elements are recycled both within the crust and between adjacent zones of our planet.

Igneous, Sedimentary and Metamorphic Rocks

Within the rock cycle three separate families of rocks are identified: igneous rocks that have crystallized from magma; sedimentary rocks, made up of particles of pre-existing rocks and laid down in layers, and metamorphic rocks that have formed at elevated temperatures and pressures, through recrystallization of previously formed rocks. The main rock types within each family are outlined below and a guide to their field identification is provided by **Tables 6.2, 6.3** and **6.4**. The schemes are simplified and include only those rocks that may be expected in the significant alpine environments. In many cases rock names can only be applied broadly in the field, requiring confirmation in the laboratory using microscopic examination and geochemical analysis. A hand lens is helpful to aid visual inspection, and dilute hydrochloric acid is useful to identify rocks containing carbonate minerals.

Silicate minerals and silica are the basic building blocks of all these rocks. Feldspar and quartz are the commonest of these rock-forming minerals, at 51 per cent and 12 per cent respectively. Next come the common dark-coloured, or *ferromagnesian* (named after the iron and magnesium they contain) minerals:

	Generally light-coloured rocks		Generally dark-coloured rocks			
	Content of dark-coloured (ferromagnesian) minerals					
	Typically 5-10%		Typically 30-50%		90% or more	
	Quartz conspicuous	Quartz rare or absent	Amphibole (Hornblende) conspicuous	Pyroxene or pyroxene and olivine conspicuous	Combinations of olivine, pyroxene and hornblende	Serpentine minerals
Coarse-grained (crystals readily visible to the naked eye – generally more than 2 mm)	Granite	Syenite	Diorite	Gabbro	Ultramafic rock (Peridotite, Pyroxenite, Hornblendite)	Serpentinite
Medium-grained (crystals just visible to the naked eye or under a hand lens – between 0.25 and 2 mm)	Microgranite	Microsyenite	Microdiorite	Dolerite		
Fine-grained (crystals not visible to the naked eye – less than 0.25 mm)	Rhyolite	Trachyte	Andesite	Basalt		
	Generally pale-coloured rocks. Rhyolite may contain visible quartz as phenocrysts.		Generally medium- to dark-coloured rocks: andesites are on average paler than basalts but there are exceptions. If phenocrysts of olivine are present the rock is probably basalt. Hornblende phenocrysts suggest andesite.			
	Obsidian is black					
Rock is glassy	Obsidian					

Table 6.2:
Field identification of
igneous rocks.

87

pyroxene (11 per cent), amphibole (5 per cent) and olivine (3 per cent). Lastly, micas and clay minerals each constitute 5 per cent, and calcite only 1 per cent. All remaining minerals are found only in minute quantities.

Igneous rocks, which have crystallized from magma, are made up of tightly interlocking crystals. This is most clearly seen in rocks such as granite, in which crystals have grown to a large size, usually within large bodies of magma that have cooled very slowly, deep in the Earth's crust. More rapid cooling of magma, nearer to the Earth's surface, results in finer-grained rocks, such as basalt. Some of the finer-grained rock varieties contain suspended larger crystals, a texture that is referred to as porphyritic. In these rocks, crystallization commenced at deep levels in the crust, but later the rocks rose to higher levels, where they cooled more rapidly. Lava chills very rapidly and, as a result, sometimes a natural glass, such as obsidian, may form.

Igneous rocks are named according to both the proportions of the main minerals present and the size of the crystals. The minerals present clearly bear a direct relationship to the chemical composition of the rock. Those rocks that are rich in silica are said to be acid, and may contain quartz. By contrast, those said to be basic contain less silica and are rich in iron and magnesium, elements characteristic of minerals such as olivine and pyroxene. (Incidentally, it is important to realize that the concept of acid and basic in these rocks is unrelated to the terms 'acid' and 'base' as they are commonly used in chemistry.) The identification of igneous rocks in the field is sometimes quite difficult, particularly if the rock is fine-grained. A simplified scheme based on the features described above is shown in **Table 6.2**; in many of the rocks, colour may prove to be a useful guide to composition.

The average size of crystals dictates which row, in Table 6.2, the rock belongs to. The general colour of medium- and fine-grained rocks is a guide to the content of dark minerals; use the other minerals to classify the rock further. In some examples of diorite and gabbro a very small amount of quartz (less than 5 per cent) may be visible under a hand lens. Serpentinite is not strictly an igneous rock: it is an ultramafic rock (that is, a rock of mantle origin) in which the olivine, pyroxene and/or hornblende have been altered to serpentine minerals.

Sedimentary rocks differ significantly from the igneous rocks because they are laid down in layers (beds) by wind, ice and water. Many sedimentary rocks are made up of fragments of pre-existing rocks and minerals. These are clearly seen in sandstone and conglomerate, for example. Many sedimentary rocks contain fossils, the remains of past life; coal and some limestones are most obviously composed of organic materials. Many limestones are chemical precipitates, as are rocksalt and gypsum-rock. Criteria for recognizing the common rocks of this group in the field are given in **Table 6.3**.

A. Clastic rocks These consist of fragments derived from pre-existing rocks, and are named according to the size of the fragments they contain.	
Conglomerate	Composed of rounded grains that are more than 2 mm in diameter.
Breccia	As conglomerate, but grains are angular.
Sandstone	Grains less than 2 mm diameter, but visible with the naked eye. Sandstones vary in composition, from those composed entirely of quartz grains to those entirely made from rock grains; some sandstones contain fragments of feldspar. *Greywacke* denotes a sandstone composed of rock grains set in a finer-grained matrix.
Mudstone	*Siltstone* has grains only visible with a x 10 hand lens; mostly very thinly bedded. *Claystone* has grains not visible with a hand lens; mostly very thinly bedded. *Shale* often denotes a mudstone that readily splits into small fragments along very thin bedding.
B. Carbonate rocks These are made up of calcium carbonate (mostly calcite) or calcium-magnesium carbonate (dolomite), or from a mixture of both; may be difficult to distinguish in the field (both will scratch with a steel penknife); limestone will effervesce strongly with dilute hydrochloric acid, whereas dolostone will only effervesce if it is first powdered.	
Limestone	Many limestones are mostly composed of very fine-grained calcium carbonate; may contain coarser-grained patches; lime-mudstones are very common; may contain variable amounts of fossils or fossil fragments; some limestones are composed of spherical or ellipsoidal pellets (ooliths); *Chalk* is a pure, soft, very fine-grained limestone.
Dolostone 'dolomite'	Typically saccharoidal in appearance, with rough broken surface; typically occurs with limestone.
C. Siliceous rocks These are made of extremely fine-grained silica; rock will scratch a steel penknife blade.	
Chert	Grey or brownish, with a flattish broken surface; occurs in masses and beds, typically with limestone.
Flint	Typically grey to black with a white exterior; breaks with curved surfaces; occurs as nodules in some abundance in parts of the Chalk.

Table 6.3:
Field identification of
sedimentary rocks.

Metamorphic rocks are formed when heat and pressure deep in the Earth's crust progressively reconstitute both igneous and sedimentary rocks, forming a new set of minerals. Crystals in many, but not all, of these rocks are visible to the naked eye and many of the rocks have a conspicuous platy texture, caused by the parallel alignment of the newly formed minerals, such as mica (**Table 6.4**). The change may be illustrated by the metamorphism of mudstone, in which intense pressure causes platy, very fine-grained white mica to grow and become aligned in the mudstone, eventually producing a very close parting (called cleavage), along which the rock (at this point, now commonly called 'slate') readily splits. Sedimentary layers are often still visible on cleavage surfaces, and indicate the original nature of the rock. As pressure and/or temperature increase, the size of the mica crystals becomes larger, and the cleavage surfaces take on a silky sheen. Still further growth forms a schistose texture in which the mica crystals become sufficiently large to be readily seen, and the rock has a new structure, or foliation.

Heat from a body of magma emplaced into the crust may also re-crystallize rocks. Heat conducted into adjacent rocks forms hornfels, a tough, very finely crystalline rock (see Table 6.4).

Rocks and Landscape

Many of the major arctic-alpine plant regions are in the, geologically speaking, relatively young mountain belts. These include the vast group of mountain ranges, built during the last 70 million years or so, that extends across Europe and much of Asia from the Cantabrian Mountains of northern Spain, to the eastern end of the Himalaya system in south-western Yunnan. Additionally, the South American Andes and the mountains of the western USA and Canada have continued to grow over a much longer period. Rocks of various types and ages are exposed in all these regions. By contrast, a few arctic-alpine regions are situated in the relicts of older mountain belts. For example, the mountains of the Scottish Highlands and Scandinavia are part of the Caledonian mountain belt, at least 400 million years old; by now these mountains have been eroded down to their cores, and are generally composed largely of metamorphic rocks.

Variation in the durability of the different rock types, and the structures found in them (bedding, cleavage, joints and faults), effectively controls the development of the landscape, since a fascinating variety of landforms is sculpted from rocks by the eroding forces of water, ice and wind. In the arctic and alpine regions, rock outcrops may be partially buried by spreads of unconsolidated superficial deposits, such as glacial, river and scree deposits, to produce a naturally mixed, and relatively bare landscape compared to more amenable climates in

Common metamorphic rocks	
Psammite	Composed of more than 80 per cent feldspar and quartz, commonly with some mica; texture weakly schistose or gneissose. A metamorphic rock containing more than 80 per cent quartz is often referred to as a quartzite.
Semipelite	Composed of 60-80 per cent feldspar and quartz; other minerals present are mica, typically with garnet and aluminium silicates such as kyanite, staurolite and sillimanite; texture may be schistose or gneissose (see 'Terms' below).
Pelite	As semipelite, but less than 60 per cent quartz and feldspar; texture may be slaty, schistose or gneissose (see below).
Amphibolite	Medium- to coarse-grained rock composed of the minerals hornblende and feldspar; may have a marked alignment of hornblende prisms; originally a basic igneous rock such as basalt or dolerite.
Marble	Metamorphosed carbonate rocks. Pure limestones recrystallize to a mosaic of coarse calcite crystals; pure dolostones recrystallize to a medium mosaic of dolomite that typically weathers creamy brown. When metamorphosed, dolostones and limestones that originally contained some mud will form attractive variegated rocks composed of various calcium and magnesium silicates.
Terms describing the texture of metamorphic rocks 'Schist', 'gneiss' and 'slate' are commonly used as names for metamorphic rocks, but are in fact descriptions of textures displayed by them.	
Slaty	Very fine-grained; readily splits along well-developed cleavage.
Schistose	Medium-grained; has parallel orientation of elongate or platy minerals, splits readily into flakes.
Gneissose	Medium to coarse-grained; irregularly banded with distinct layers of contrasting minerals and texture, layers typically more than 5 mm wide.
Metamorphic rocks adjacent to igneous intrusions	
Hornfels	Tough crystalline rock in which individual crystals are hardly visible, even with a hand lens; former mudstone may contain aluminium silicates (andalusite and/or cordierite).

Table 6.4:
Field identification of the most common metamorphic rocks. (Proportions of minerals present may be estimated visually.)

which soils have developed on the drift deposits and weathered rock. In these areas, stark scenery merges into a vegetated landscape containing a wide variety of plant habitats. Lastly, few landscapes have escaped man's activities: the stability of steep mountainsides is significantly threatened by forest clear-cutting, and this leads to soil erosion and landslides.

Igneous Rock Landscapes

Volcanoes form significant alpine areas, particularly those of the western side of North and South America, while Iceland is entirely volcanic. These dramatic constructional landforms are often typified by nearly perfect geometrical cones. Soils develop only on the lower flanks of the volcano, where the risk of burial from further ash fallout is low (**Plate 6.2**). Nearer to the summit the slopes are typically composed of bare lava and ash. These blankets of ash experience acute drainage, but individual ash particles are commonly riddled with small holes (vesicles), and are thus capable of retaining considerable amounts of water for use by plants growing in these conditions. And, because the ash is abundantly vesicular, each particle has a relatively large surface area (compared with a solid rock fragment of similar size), thus allowing the process of chemical weathering to release nutrients that are essential for the plants.

Landscapes underlain by coarse-grained igneous rocks such as granite are fashioned by chemical weathering of the constituent minerals. The common form of granite landscape, exemplified by the Cairngorm massif in the Grampian Highlands in Scotland, is controlled by the frequency and spacing of the three joint sets: typically, two joints are near-vertical while the other is horizontal.

Left: 6.2 Volcanic landscape of Mt Rainier, Washington State, USA. Lower slopes are intensely vegetated with soils well developed and a low risk of burial or disruption from all but the largest volcanic eruptions. With higher altitude soil development is typically incomplete and there is greater risk of disruption or burial during eruptions.

Sedimentary Rock Landscapes

Sedimentary rocks form much of the thin, surface skin of the Earth. They may occur as massifs, largely composed of limestone or sandstone, or more typically in mixed sequences (of sandstone and mudstone, for example). The Southern Uplands of Scotland, typified by smooth steep, convex-shaped hills, are a fine example of a landscape that has formed predominantly from a single rock type – in this case, greywacke. Conversely, landscape formed in areas of mixed sedimentary rocks typically consists of steep ridges separated by benches and hollows (**Plate 6.3**). These features are formed from layers of resistant, hard strata (such as sandstone or limestone), which may be exposed along the upstanding ridges and benches, in alternation with softer strata (such as mudstone, or poorly cemented sandstone) that form the hollows in between. Where the strata lie horizontally, the table-top and layer-cake geology forms magnificent valley-side landscapes, such as the Yorkshire Dales. Where the strata are tilted, a dip and scarp landscape results, as seen in the Welsh Borderland and around Hadrian's Wall in Northumberland; here, cliffs formed by the harder layers dip gently back to hollows in the softer strata. In mountain terrains, sedimentary rocks are commonly folded and contorted; some spectacular examples are displayed in parts of the Alps.

Karst Landforms

Carbonate rocks form up to 20 per cent of rocks exposed at the Earth's surface, and the substantial, carbonate-rich massifs within the Alpine-Himalayan mountain belt are noted for their abundant and diverse flora. Examples, all of which have featured in the Bulletin of the Alpine Garden Society, include the Dolomites of northern Italy, the Pindhos Mountains (**Plate 6.4**), Mount Olympus in northern Greece and the Yulong Shan and Beima Shan in Yunnan (in the south-west of China).

Above left: 6.3 Sedimentary rock landscape in the upper Magdalena valley, Colombia. A sequence of sandstones intercalated with thin beds of mudstone form the series of stepped features seen in the foreground; the beds dip from right to left. The softer mudstone units are more readily eroded to form sloping benches, while the more durable sandstone forms the scarps.

Above right: 6.4 Limestone landscape in the Pindhos Mountains of northern Greece.

All these areas have distinctive landforms, known as 'karst', created by the effects of slightly acidic rainwater slowly dissolving the limestone. Many limestones contain little that is insoluble, and hence their soils are generally very thin, or completely absent over many parts. Thick residual deposits are present only locally, where they have developed over long periods from minute amounts of impurities that accumulate to produce rendzina, or terra rossa. Limestone pavements are a typical feature, with excellent examples in the Carboniferous limestones of northern England and the Burren in Ireland. A pattern of relatively flat surfaces (clints) is separated by deep grooves (grikes) that have developed where dissolution has widened the joints.

Dry valleys and spectacular gorges are also significant features of karst, where water movement is usually underground through interconnected joints that are widened by solution, and through concealed rivers and cave systems, often impressive. The only surface water on many of these massifs either originates from snow and ice melt, or has come from streams that originate outside the limestone areas; these streams probably only survive on the surface because their volume of flow exceeds the amount of seepage into underground routes. In areas of warm, humid climate with high rainfall, rapid rates of dissolution of the limestone produce spectacular vertical grooves in the crags ('pinnacle' karst). Dramatic steep-sided mountains with gorges and broad alluvial valleys form 'tower' karst, with good examples at Guilin, in south-west China, and elsewhere in south-east Asia.

Metamorphic Rock Landscapes

Metamorphic rocks occur as zones within the younger mountain belts such as the Alps and the Himalayas. However, they also form a very substantial proportion of the older mountain belts, such as the Scottish Highlands and mountains of Scandinavia. These ranges have undergone more than 400 million years of uplift and erosion, thus exposing much deeper levels within their core than younger mountain areas.

Many metamorphic rocks are jointed, possess a layering akin to the bedding in sedimentary rock and produce similar landforms. This is particularly so where the metamorphic rocks were originally sedimentary, before their transformation. Most of the metamorphic rocks are hard and resistant to solution and weathering, and so produce thin, acid soils that are lacking in nutrients. Commonly, these landscapes have poor drainage and are covered with a blanket of peat that has formed since the melting of the last ice sheets. However, despite this, metamorphosed calcareous rocks in the Breadalbane mountains, in Perthshire, are home to some of Britain's richest alpine floras.

Glaciated Landforms

Ice has sculpted rock in many arctic-alpine areas, even those at the equator. Precipitous rock amphitheatres (called 'cirques' in France, 'corries' in Scotland, 'cwms' in Wales and 'combes' in the Lake District) form at the head of valleys, and merge to leave jagged rock peaks or 'horns' (the Matterhorn being a prime example) and arêtes (knife-edge ridges). The typical steep-sided, flat-bottomed glaciated valleys result from a combination of erosion by glaciers and deposits left as they melted. Spreads of moraine are deposited from valley glaciers along the valley sides and as arcuate hummocky ridges at the snout of the ice. Moraine varies in composition from a stiff stony clay to sand and gravel; thus ground conditions may vary from boggy to extremely well drained (**Plate 6.5**). When larger ice sheets melt the process leaves a blanket of till, smeared across the landscape. Till is composed of rock fragments of all sizes, set in a stiff sandy clay matrix (**Plate 6.6**), and thick spreads of glacial till often form into collections of whale-shaped mounds, called drumlins. Many alpine meadows develop on spreads of glacial till. Sediment is transported away from these areas by torrential meltwater streams, which build up spreads of alluvial sand and gravel. Outside of the immediate glacial environment, rocky mountain tops are eroded by frost action and the wind to leave an accumulation of rock fragments, rock powder and resistant minerals, such as quartz, while fragments of frost-broken rock form aprons of scree beneath crags.

Top right: 6.5 The Gangapurna glacier, Annapurna range, near Manang, Nepal. This temperate valley glacier has retreated significantly from its maximum extent in the foreground of the picture. The steep-sided ridges along the valley side and projecting into the main valley are moraines, in this case composed variably of stony sandy clay and sand and gravel. The slopes are unstable and subject to slumping during the monsoon season and during periods of freeze-thaw; note the lake and outflow stream.

Bottom right: 6.6 *Androsace mariae* growing in till, near Huanglongsi, Sichuan, China. The till contains fragments of limestone and other rocks within a stiff sandy clay matrix.

River Deposits

Mountain ranges are dissected by fast-flowing rivers, whose progress both erodes the rock and transports vast volumes of sediment. Though long stretches of the river course may be along narrow, deep gorges, elsewhere the river gradient may be gentler, and the valley wider. During periodic flooding in these areas the sediment transported by the river is left behind, as alluvial deposits of gravel, sand, silt or clay, and forms a flat flood-plain. Though prone to further inundation, flood-plains form significant floral habitats because of the sharp drainage provided by the deposits of gravel and sand, and the fertile soils that develop on silts and clays. Spreads of gravel are very uneven in composition because of shifting stream courses; the gravel is largely composed of angular to well-rounded fragments of different rock types, which reflect the overall geology of the river catchment area.

In mountainous areas the confluence of tributary streams is marked by aprons of alluvial gravel and sand. These alluvial fans accumulate because the constricted tributary streams become unable to carry their huge volumes of sediment once their velocity is abruptly reduced on reaching the outlet into the wider main valley.

Weathering

The Earth's surface is an environment characterized by an oxygen-rich atmosphere and, in all but arid areas, by water. Both contribute to the conditions under which rocks 'weather' and, as a result, disintegrate. Weathering may initially involve the mechanical break up of rocks into smaller particles – a process referred to as physical weathering. Subsequently, rocks are subject to chemical weathering and breakdown. Biological agents also contribute to both types of weathering: mechanical breakdown may be aided by the growth of large root systems while chemical attack may occur through, for example, acids, both from lichens and in soils. Once weathered, rock is more readily eroded by water, ice or wind. However, weathering products themselves may accumulate to form a blanket of residual deposits that, with the additional influence of organic materials, are transformed to soil at its surface. Weathering therefore provides the chemical basis for soils and is the essential first step in soil formation (**Plate 6.7**).

There is very little chemical weathering in constantly cold and dry regions, where the main agent is physical weathering. By contrast, in moist regions chemical weathering is predominant. In mountain environments recent glaciations and rapid rates of erosion have commonly resulted in the widespread removal of soils. In mountain terrains the erosional agents (water, wind and ice) redistribute the weathering products to form great spreads of alluvial and lacustrine deposits, loess (wind-laid silt), scree, till and moraine. Furthermore, and partly as

Left: 6.7 *Onosma bracteata*, Thorong La, Nepal. The plant is growing in scree composed of a mixture of fragments of limestone and mudstone. Exposure to freeze-thaw and abundant moisture has resulted in the complete disintegration of the mudstone fragments to form the basic mineral element of a soil.

a result of this, there has been insufficient time for the redevelopment of soils on all but very old moraines and stabilized screes. However, exposure of the rocks to ice and water over long periods results in many rocks having a rotten appearance: original structures and mineral grains are sometimes still visible in the rock, even though it may be friable to the touch.

Physical Weathering

As rocks become exposed at the Earth's surface, stresses are released, and naturally formed fractures in the rocks gradually open. In the arctic-alpine environment the rapid freezing and thawing of ice is a very potent agent in the physical breakdown of rock, particularly in areas where there are large diurnal changes in temperature. Water invades even the narrowest of fractures in the rock and freezes at night, only to thaw again the next morning. When water freezes to form ice there is an increase in volume of 9 per cent, and in confined spaces this may exert sufficient pressure to exceed the strength of the rock. However, it is also thought that very large hydraulic pressures may be generated during the freezing process, when still unfrozen water is displaced away from the advancing ice front. Rock fragments liberated by the freeze-thaw process may litter the mountain tops and collect beneath crags to form screes. The opening of fractures by this means provides an increased surface area for the penetrative effect of chemical agents.

Chemical Weathering

Many rock-forming minerals, particularly those that constitute coarse-grained igneous and metamorphic rocks, crystallized at temperatures and pressures that were far higher than those at the Earth's surface. Now at the surface, they are naturally unstable in this relatively new environment, and over time will begin to break down. Although pure water will dissolve most natural substances, given sufficient time, this process is accelerated by the slight acidity of most rain and ground water due to the presence, in solution, of carbon dioxide from the air. Chemical weathering of this kind contributes to the disintegration of rocks in a number of ways, and the effects can often be seen on the rock surface. Once chemical weathering has weakened the coherence between adjacent mineral grains, these become susceptible to removal by other agents. Solutions are formed and washed out of the rock by rain, thus rendering the rock more porous; the rock becomes weaker and there is a greater surface area available for chemical attack. New minerals formed during chemical weathering typically have larger volumes than those they replace, causing the outer shell of rock to swell and pull away from the inner part.

Perhaps the simplest of all chemical weathering processes is that of solution, which principally affects those carbonate rocks that are most easily weathered, and has already been described in relation to the development of karst landforms. Solution is most rapid in areas where soil cover has developed due to the higher levels of carbon dioxide present as a result of microbial activity.

The ease with which the other common rock-forming minerals decompose varies. Feldspars readily react with water through a process called hydrolysis. The calcium, potassium and sodium in the feldspar are taken into solution as carbonates and chlorides, and silica is liberated as silicic acid. New, stable, aluminium silicate 'clay' minerals, such as kaolinite and montmorillonite, are then formed. Some of the potassium is adsorbed (held on the surface) by the clay minerals and ultimately may be released to plants. Brown mica (biotite) is very susceptible to decomposition, as are olivine, pyroxene and amphibole. In these minerals the magnesium, calcium and iron form carbonates and chlorides, and are removed in solution. Some of the iron oxidizes and gives a reddish-brown coloration to any residual deposit. The aluminium and silica go to form clay minerals, though some silica may form a colloidal solution and is removed. Another important element required by plants is phosphorus, which occurs in the minerals apatite and monazite and is seen in very small quantities in most rocks. Apatite is readily altered and is soluble in acidulated waters while, on the other hand, monazite is very resistant to alteration, and is typically present as detrital minerals in sedimentary rocks. Phosphorus is concentrated by bony, and some shelly, organisms. Finally, quartz and white mica (muscovite) are extremely resistant to decomposition.

Residual Deposits

Basic igneous rocks are entirely composed of feldspar, olivine, pyroxene and amphibole; since these minerals readily alter to clay minerals, the rocks are commonly wholly decomposed by chemical weathering. Large quantities of iron oxides and hydroxides, and abundant clay minerals, form thick blankets of distinctive brown and red clay deposits, particularly in humid climates. Basic rocks will thus weather more rapidly than acid igneous rocks, which contain substantial amounts of the resistant minerals, quartz and white mica. Residual deposits from the chemical breakdown of acid igneous rocks will largely consist of quartz grains mixed with an accumulation of white mica and clay. Metamorphic rocks that are rich in quartz and muscovite will be very resistant to weathering, although calcareous metamorphic rocks – for example those of the Scottish Highlands – weather comparatively easily.

Detrital sedimentary rocks, such as sandstone and mudstone, are composed primarily of quartz and clays that are themselves products of the breakdown of other rocks, and might be expected to resist chemical weathering. However, on weathering the clay minerals commonly adsorb more water, with a consequent increase in volume and disintegration. Minerals such as carbonate, which may cement the grains together, are readily removed in solution, leaving behind a residue of loose sand. By contrast, those sedimentary rocks cemented with silica are virtually indestructible except by mechanical breakdown. Sedimentary rocks typically have abundant partings parallel to bedding, and joints; both are readily attacked by regular frost action, and thus are broken down mechanically in the alpine environment.

Most limestones and dolostones contain very little else apart from carbonate minerals, which are readily removed in solution. Thus, there is little residual material to form the basis of soils. However, trace concentrations of iron in the carbonate minerals may accumulate with time to produce a residual deposit rich in iron hydroxides; this is the well known terra rossa (red earth) found in limestone areas of the eastern Mediterranean region, for example.

Soils

Soils have three chief functions in relation to plant growth: physical support, water supply and nutrient supply. Physical support for the root system enables the plant to anchor itself, which is essential, in most species, for growth and reproduction. Having anchored themselves, alpine plants must acquire their water and essential nutrient supply from substrates that differ, in many respects, from those common at lower altitudes. In general, alpine soils do not have the well-developed layered structure typical of soils in other climates. Because chemical weathering is retarded in cold conditions, the parent rock or superficial deposit is weakly oxidized, and the clay-enriched B horizon (see Glossary) that is so typical of temperate lowland soils is generally absent. Alpine soils vary widely over short distances, which often results in a patchy mosaic of soil types that are weakly developed on till, moraine, scree and fine, wind-blown material. Organic-rich layers characterize poorly drained areas and peat bogs. Soil profiles with recognizable A and B horizons are only developed beneath long-established alpine meadows. Vegetation mosaics closely mirror these below-ground soil patterns, thus indicating the tight link between soils and plant distribution in alpine ecosystems.

Physical Processes that Assist Alpine Soil Formation

As discussed above, the combined processes of rock erosion and physical and chemical weathering initiate the process of soil development in alpine terrain. Three other processes are also involved:

1. Gravitational processes on and below slopes, leading to movement and accumulation of soil-forming materials.
2. The carrying of soil-forming materials by snow and ice (avalanches, glaciers, and water.
3. Wind dispersion and sedimentation of fine materials.

In addition, freeze-thaw cycles may play an important part in any of these processes. In general, soil formation starts with the deposit of finer materials onto a coarser matrix, such as scree or moraine. The fine material normally accumulates from the bottom up, and may not reach the surface for a long time, if at all, and thus is generally hidden from view, except in the oldest and most well-developed examples. Nevertheless, deep down among the stones there may be a good depth of fine material that can support a surprisingly rich flora. Also, although the stones on a south-facing scree may themselves be hot and dry, deeper down below the surface there is generally a continuous supply of cool moisture. This can be easily demonstrated on a scree that is not too deep, by stripping off the top layers of coarse material. Just as a surface dressing of chippings on a pot plant reduces moisture loss from the compost, so the stones on the scree's surface screen the substrate beneath from direct heating and evaporation. While the cooling effect is beneficial to plants growing on south-facing screes, it may result in north-facing screes at high elevations actually being too cold for plant growth; the roots have to grow deep, and so lose the advantage of any radiant soil warming that they might receive nearer the surface.

Wind plays an important part in the development of alpine soils. While windblown dust is normally only associated with dryland areas in the lowlands, it does occur everywhere in the mountains. The continual supply of silt- and clay-sized particles is provided mainly from glacial deposits. These are often made on snow, subsequently released when it melts, and thereafter either remain in situ or are redistributed by mountain winds. A study in the Alps revealed that, on average, 70-80 g (2½-3 oz) of mineral dust is deposited per square metre during the period of snow cover, and 15-30 g (½-1 oz) in summer, giving a total of about 1 tonne per hectare per year (0.4 tonne per acre per year) (Gruber 1980, quoted in Körner 1999). The lower of these rates of deposition would result in the accumulation of 10 cm (4 in) of fine substrate during the approximately 10,000 years since the last glaciation, but only if (and it is a big 'if') it had all remained in situ. Accumulation rates may be much faster in drier and windier mountain ranges.

The transportation of soil-forming materials by wind is not necessarily restricted to short distances. Dust may be carried from far afield; for example from areas of one rock assemblage to another. In the same study Gruber (1980) calculated that the annual addition of calcium carbonate in dust to vegetation growing on non-calcareous formations ranged from 12-1,100 kg (26-2,400 lb) per hectare per year. Values as high as 100 kg (220 lb) per hectare per year were found in places at least 5 km (3 miles) distant from the nearest upwind point source.

The depth of wind-blown material that accumulates in any one place is dependent on relief and plant cover. Dust accumulates most rapidly in depressions, in sheltered locations among large stones and boulders and also around vegetation that is able to trap it, especially shrubs.

The average particle size of mineral material in alpine soils varies with rock type and elevation. Siliceous rocks (sandstone and, especially, granite and psammite) produce a coarser initial grain structure than calcareous rocks and thus the soils formed from them tend to be more open in structure and more freely drained. Grain size also tends to increase with elevation, regardless of geology, because there has been less opportunity for weathering high up among the rocks. This point is of significance for the gardener as it explains, in part, why plants from the highest elevations tend to demand the most free-draining composts in cultivation.

As well as playing an important part in the physical weathering of rocks, as described earlier in this chapter, alternate freezing and thawing also aid the breaking and mixing of soil particles in mature soils. Soil heave (expansion and contraction of sediments) also aerates the nascent soil. In addition, soil creep – associated with freeze-thaw, and often exacerbated by summer rain and snowmelt – is a common phenomenon on slopes. At times, soil conditions may result in large-scale flow of considerable masses of soil and rock debris – a process referred to as solifluction, and particularly characteristic of areas of permafrost. Mark (1994) found that soil creep occurred even on shallow (3-7 degrees) slopes on the Old Man Range, in New Zealand, with downhill soil movement averaging 0.35 cm (⅛ in) per year. Soil creep occurred even on quite heavily vegetated soils, but not under the densest plant cover. It is unclear whether soil creep eventually ceases because increasing vegetation cover stabilizes the soil, or if vegetation increases because the stripes become inactive. The degree to which plant survival is affected by soil heaving, and subsequent soil creep, depends on the rate of soil movement. On steep slopes, with mobile soil material and a constant supply of water, creep may be so rapid that only specialist plants are able to survive the mechanical tensions. These plants are usually either those with deep and elastic roots that are difficult to prise out of the ground or break (for example many rosette plants), or those having rhizomes that are easily broken, but which have a high potential for root regeneration (for example, many campanulas, sedums and grasses).

Much of the puzzling patterned ground found in the mountains (stripes, polygons, frost hummocks etc.) is also caused by freeze-thaw processes. These patterns often underlie substantial small-scale patterning of the vegetation because they arise from differences in soil depth, drainage and nutrient content. They may also affect the localized depth and duration of snow cover (see Chapter 5).

Permafrost occurs in high mountains as well as in the Arctic. However, while arctic permafrost is generally continuous over large areas, alpine permafrost is often patchy. The line of continuous alpine permafrost, where it occurs, generally matches the line of the upper limit of higher plant distribution (Lawler 1988). At temperate latitudes, on poleward-facing slopes, permafrost may reach down as far as the tree line, but here the ice is generally too far below the soil surface to interfere directly with plant growth. An exception to this has been found by Fahey (1974) in Colorado fellfields, where permanent ice occurred at the tree line at much shallower depths. The effects of permafrost on plant survival and growth are fully discussed in Chapter 4.

Soil Organic Matter

The physical and chemical processes described above create a fine-grain mineral material in which plant roots can grow and obtain both water and whatever nutrients are present. Whether such substrates can be called soils is a matter for debate, since a normal component of soil, as we think of it, is organic matter – and these materials contain little, or none. Nevertheless, over vast tracts of mountain terrain, subject to constant disturbance by wind and water erosion, freeze-thaw and landslide, unstructured mineral substrates are all there is for plants to grow in. Yet many of our choicest alpines not only grow but thrive in these unpromising materials. How do they manage it? Recent research (Körner 1993) has shown that, in the case of cushion plants at least, dead, nutrient-rich organic matter is accumulated within the dense body of the plant, thus allowing it to partly uncouple itself from the substrate in which it is growing. A highly conservative nutrient recycling regime is established, involving a rich microflora in an otherwise hostile soil environment. This being the case, when observing plants growing in the wild one should take care not to jump to the conclusion that they must be getting everything they need from the soil.

Where mineral soil-forming materials do have a chance to settle and accumulate, and hence develop a denser vegetation cover, dead plant material will also accumulate and the process of soil development through the incorporation of organic matter will begin. This may occur over large areas on flat ground, or shallow slopes or in deep rock crevices. In such situations the amount of organic matter in well-developed soil may actually be much higher than in lowland soils, even though the amount of dead litter and roots contributing to its formation is actually much less. This is because the rate of decay of organic matter, like all other biochemical processes, is controlled by temperature. At higher elevations temperature decreases, and so does the rate of decomposition. A leaf that would take less than a year to decompose completely in a lowland soil might take two years or more to do so in a montane soil. Again, this has implications for the cultivation of high alpines. In the wild, many species grow in well-developed alpine soils having high soil organic matter content (this includes many ledge and crevice plants, as well as woodland and alpine meadow dwellers). But the organic matter decomposes slowly, meaning that the mineral nutrients it contains, especially nitrogen, are released slowly. This is unlike the situation in the garden, where organic matter decomposition and nutrient release both occur at a much faster rate. All too often in cultivation the result can be overfed plants that are out of character, and which often produce more foliage and fewer flowers than those growing in the wild.

Unfortunately, it is not possible to reduce soil organic matter decomposition rates in cultivation by reducing soil temperatures unless one either reduces light levels (generally undesirable for high alpines) or provides artificial soil cooling (as in the alpine house at Kew). However the problem can be minimized by reducing the organic matter of the soil or compost, ensuring that it is free draining – so that nutrients released in excess of the plant's requirements are quickly washed away by rain or irrigation water.

It should be noted that the accumulation and subsequent turnover of dead plant and animal material in soil alters not only its structure and capacity to hold and release nutrients, but also leads to soil acidification. Plant and animal remains acidify the soil, the process being most marked in cold and moist environments where recycling is slowest. Humic acids formed by decay of soil organic matter peak early in the growing season, and seep down into the lower soil layers through the summer. As they pass downwards these acids are neutralized by the basic ions in the soil, primarily calcium and magnesium. But if there are insufficient calcium and magnesium ions available the soil will gradually become more acid. In this case ions such as manganese and aluminium will be released into the soil solution, and may reach concentrations that would be toxic to lowland plants. Clearly, alpines growing in such soils will need to be tolerant of high concentrations of heavy metals in the soil solution. That many are tolerant is shown by the species-rich alpine plant communities often found in such unpromising situations.

In arid mountains this process of soil acidification is much less important, and may be absent. Less plant biomass is generally produced due to moisture limitation of growth so less dead material is available for incorporation into the soil. The shortage of soil organic matter and soil moisture in turn hinders the formation of humic acids. These very dry soils may never develop an appreciable organic matter content, and may appear structureless and lifeless when examined. Nevertheless, while their plant cover is usually much sparser than that of soils in more mesic (less arid) mountain environments, there are specialist plant species that have evolved to cope with these conditions. Cacti (of which there are a good many montane species) come immediately to mind, but there are many other more typically alpine plants, such as the rosulate violas of the Andes, and the numerous species of *Astragalus* characteristically inhabiting the dry mountains of Eurasia and the Americas.

7·CHEMICAL NUTRITION OF ALPINE PLANTS

The essential chemical elements required for plant growth come mostly from the soil, as described in Chapter 6, although some may be obtained from snowmelt water, as mentioned in Chapter 5, or from dust deposited from the atmosphere. Essential nutrients are likely to be available in a less balanced, and more variable, supply in 'young' and often poorly developed alpine soils than in well-developed lowland soils that have a good mix of fine and coarse mineral fractions and organic matter. It might be expected, therefore, that the growth of alpines in the wild, especially in the more extreme habitats, is often limited by nutritional shortage or imbalance. However, this is not always the case.

Nitrogen

Although nitrogen (N) is an abundant element in nature (as nitrogen gas, just over 78 per cent in the air we breathe) it is, paradoxically, especially likely to be unavailable to plants. This is because higher plants cannot utilize gaseous nitrogen and, unlike the other essential nutrients, it is generally absent from mineral soil-forming materials (Vitousek and Walker 1987). The total concentration of nitrogen in alpine soils is correlated with soil organic matter (SOM) concentration. The SOM supplies nitrogen in forms that are available to plants, through the microbial decay of the dead plant and animal material from which it is composed. Depending on soil conditions the nitrogen may be available primarily either as nitrate or ammonium ions. Commonly, ammonium nitrogen dominates in organic and acid alpine soils, nitrate nitrogen in more mineral and alkaline soils.

Most of the nitrogen in soils gets there originally through a process known as biological nitrogen fixation. This involves microbes taking gaseous nitrogen from the air in the soil and converting it into organic forms. This nitrogen fixation is achieved either by bacteria living within the roots of plants or by free-living soil microbes. The former system (symbiotic nitrogen fixation) has been perfected in plants of the pea family (legumes), and is found in such alpine species as *Astragalus*, *Lupinus* and *Oxytropis*. The bacteria living in nodules on the roots receive food from the plant and, in return, provide the plant with a reliable supply of nitrogen. Once the nitrogen has been 'fixed' by the bacteria it can be remobilized when the plant's remains return to the soil and decompose. It is then available to be taken up by the roots of other plants. Accumulation of soil nitrogen in this way has been shown to be a critical factor in the development of ecosystems on bare ground in the lowlands (Marrs *et al.* 1981).

Until sufficient nitrogen accumulates in the soil, the development of plant communities is severely limited, and this is no less true in the mountains. At low to medium elevation, symbiotic nitrogen-fixation commonly plays an important role in nitrogen accumulation while at higher elevations, symbiotic nitrogen-fixation features less, and nitrogen-fixation by free-living cyanobacteria (a type of bacteria that performs photosynthesis) increases in prevalence. This is because legumes feature less in floras at higher elevations, and are virtually absent from the plant communities at the highest altitudes above the snowline. Though perhaps puzzling at first sight, this may be because legumes growing at high altitudes are unable to spare the energy required to provide food for the bacteria that can perform the nitrogen-fixation.

In studies of moraines of various ages deposited in Alaska and British Columbia, it was found that total soil nitrogen increased by factors varying from between 6-fold and 45-fold during the first 100 years after the glacial retreat. In a study to determine the importance of symbiotic nitrogen fixation to this nitrogen enrichment, Blundon and Dale (1990) discovered that one species, the legume *Hedysarum boreale* var. *mackenzii* contributed 72 per cent of the nitrogen input in the pioneer stage (that is, when the first plant species began to grow), 79 per cent in the intermediate *Dryas* community stage (although *Dryas* itself, while not a legume, is also a nitrogen fixer), and 88 per cent in the final stage of succession, the Englemann spruce forests. Free-living nitrogen-fixing soil microorganisms provided most of the remaining nitrogen input. The importance of the symbiotically fixed nitrogen to the plants themselves is indicated by work of Bowman *et al.* (1996), who showed that *Trifolium* (clover) species from 3,650 metres (12,000 feet) on Niwot Ridge, Colorado, obtained 70- 100 per cent of their nitrogen requirements by symbiotic nitrogen-fixation.

Nitrogen
Nitrogen, which is required in larger amounts than any other mineral element for plant growth, is generally deficient in newly-formed mineral soils. This is because nitrogen does not occur naturally in the rocks from which the mineral soil is derived, and can only be obtained either by the decay of organic matter or by biological fixation of atmospheric nitrogen gas. As soil organic matter (SOM) gradually accumulates (a crucial part of alpine ecosystem development), so the amount of nitrogen available to plants in the form of ammonium and/or nitrate increases. Plants other than legumes (which are nitrogen-fixers) growing naturally on nitrogen-deficient mineral soils (that is, scree and rock crevice plants), have evolved to tolerate low levels of soil nitrogen. In fact they may be damaged or even killed in cultivation if exposed to levels of nitrogen that would be considered quite normal for plants (such as alpine meadow and woodland plants) that grow naturally in more fertile soils.

Yet another way in which alpine plants obtain nitrogen is by 'consuming' insects. Carnivorous plants such as butterworts (*Pinguicula* spp.) (**Plate 7.1**) and sundews (*Drosera* spp.) catch insects on their sticky leaf surfaces and secrete enzymes that digest them, subsequently absorbing the nutrients released in the process.

Some plants get some or all of their nitrogen by parasitizing the roots of other species. Examples include louseworts (*Pedicularis*) and Indian paint brushes (*Castilleja*) (**Plate 7.2**), both of which are hemiparasites (able also to perform some photosynthesis) rather than being fully parasitic on their hosts. It used to be thought that even hemiparasitic plants were impossible to grow in cultivation unless they could be persuaded to form a root association with a suitable plant, grasses often being used. But it is now clear that they can be grown perfectly satisfactorily in isolation, provided they are given abundant supplies of nitrogen. The author has found that such plants growing in the open garden, and fed fortnightly throughout the growing season with a high nitrogen fertilizer, will remain green and flower very well, but will go pale and stop growing as soon as fertilizer application is stopped.

Below left: 7.1 *Pinguicula longifolia* with insects rich in nitrogen and other nutrients trapped on the sticky leaves. Ordesa Canyon, Pyrenees.

Below right: 7.2 Castillejas, such as *C. aff rhexifolia*, are partial parasites ('hemiparasites') that take nutrients from the roots of herbs and grasses among which they grow.

There is surprisingly little information on the effects of nitrogen on arctic and alpine plant communities, or on individual species in the field, although continuing studies at Niwot Ridge, in the Front Range of Colorado, are providing some important insights. Nitrogen addition in three alpine communities brought increased foliage production but a decrease in plant diversity (Seastedt and Vaccaro 2001). But the growth response varied considerably depending on the plant community concerned and the type and level of nitrogen fertilizer applied. In general, shrubs seem to respond less than non-woody plants, and evergreen shrubs less than deciduous ones. Some plant species respond positively to low levels of nitrogen but are damaged by higher additions. Others, notably coarse grasses and short-lived annuals and biennials, often only respond to relatively high applications. It is likely that soil type and condition – major factors in determining the amounts of natural and added nitrogen available to the plants – are at least partly responsible for the conflicting results.

Theodose *et al.* (1996) made the interesting and surprising observation that those species that took up most nitrogen from the soil had no competitive advantage over other species that accumulated less. They also found that rare species, with relatively slow growth rates, took up as much or more nitrogen as common and widespread dominant species. They suggest that in harsh environments, unlike in those that are more favourable for plant growth, high uptake rates of resources such as nitrogen are in fact not indicative of competitive ability. They may instead be a mechanism by which rare species are able to coexist with plants that would normally exclude them. Yet another aspect of nitrogen nutrition was studied by Mullen *et al.* (1998), who investigated seasonal uptake of nitrogen by the snowbed buttercup, *Ranunculus adoneus*, in order to assess its ability to utilize the flush of nitrogen released during snowmelt. Nitrogen uptake mostly occurred very early in the growing season before new roots were formed, the old roots mopping up available nitrogen in the ice-cold water released by the melting snow.

It seems that high alpines, like most plants growing in open communities or on bare soils, are very efficient at searching out nutrients and retaining them. Hence nutrient concentrations in leaves of alpines in the wild are often surprisingly high, and may be higher than in plants from much more fertile soils at lower elevations. Large root systems have probably evolved partly as a means of obtaining adequate nutrients, especially nitrogen, from nutrient-deficient soils. Cushion and other dense plant life form trap litter effectively, and create very favourable micro-environments for litter-decomposing organisms and for the growth of adventitious roots that take up the nutrients and recycle them. Measurements in the field

indicate that at least 50 per cent of nitrogen and other mineral nutrients in a range of alpine plants are recycled within the vegetation in this way, without passing through the soil (**Plate 7.3**).

Above: 7.3 Long-lived cushion plants such as *Haastia pulvinaris* var. *minor* are particularly efficient at recycling nutrients derived from dead and decaying foliage.

In the buoyant, breezy atmosphere of the high mountains, to which alpine plants are perfectly adapted, these mechanisms ensure efficient nutrient recycling. But in lowland gardens with little air circulation, and especially in glasshouses and frames, they may create problems. The decaying leaves within the cushion provide ideal conditions not only for harmless decomposers, but also for harmful fungi and bacteria that the plants may never encounter in the wild, and against which they have developed no natural defences.

Cultivated garden and nursery soils and commercial potting composts generally contain much more available nitrogen than the developing soils of most arctic-alpine habitats. This can cause problems when we try to grow alpines in such soils and composts. The plants respond to the luxury supply of nitrogen, to which they are unaccustomed, by producing abundant leafy growth. This, as well as making them look out of character, is prone to insect and fungal attack or frost damage. It is worth making some comparisons of relative biomass production at this point, in order to realize just how small the absolute nutrient requirements of alpines are. A cushion alpine (such as an androsace growing in ideal conditions) would typically produce only a fraction of the biomass, over a given period of time, of a cabbage or a border chrysanthemum. It is therefore not surprising that the androsace only needs a fraction of the nutrients. By adding grit or other materials to soils and composts we improve their suitability for alpines not only by enhancing their drainage characteristics, but also by diluting nutrient levels, especially nitrogen.

Atmospheric nitrogen pollution
Nitrogen pollution emanating from fossil fuels burned in factories, homes and automobiles is being deposited in the mountains, especially those areas near centres of population. This is likely to reduce species diversity by favouring coarse, fast-growing species at the expense of slower-growing more 'choice' alpines. Unless reversed, nitrogen pollution, together with climate change (see Chapter 9), may have severe consequences for high alpine plants in highly polluted mountain regions such as the Appalachians of northeast America and the Carpathian mountains in eastern Europe.

A 'new' source of nitrogen, and one that is probably already affecting alpine plant communities (although little of the detail is yet known), is atmospheric nitrogen pollution as a result of man's burning of fossil fuels. Nitrogen oxides in vehicle exhaust fumes form an ever-increasing proportion of this pollution, and are carried far and wide – finally deposited to the ground and vegetation, both in gaseous forms and as dilute nitric and nitrous acids in rain and snow. Nowhere on the

Below: 7.4 Alpine tundra communities such as this one at Guanella Pass, Colorado, are likely to be adversely affected by increasing levels of pollutant nitrogen deposition, with decreases in species diversity as a result of increased dominance by coarse grasses and herbs.

planet is immune from this atmospheric nitrogen input, but those mountains closest to centres of population and industry are affected more than those in regions remote from man's activities. The amounts of nitrogen deposited from the atmosphere to alpine ecosystems vary from <5 to > 20 kilograms (<11 to > 44 lbs) per hectare per year. It is likely that nitrogen additions in the upper part of this range will have a significant impact on alpine plant communities. Bowman and Steltzer (1998) conclude that in the alpine tundra in the southern Rocky Mountains (**Plate 7.4**), which is receiving 8-10 kg (18-22 lbs) of nitrogen per hectare per year, there will be changes in plant species composition as a result of competitive displacement. Species diversity is likely to decrease as a wide range of slower growing herbs and shrubs, which are relatively unresponsive to nitrogen, are replaced by a small selection of responsive coarse herbs and grasses. Unfortunately, most of the alpines we value most highly today as garden plants fall into the threatened category.

Apart from nitrogen, the other essential nutrients come, in the wild, from various sources. These are primarily weathering of rocks and finer mineral particles (see Chapter 6 for details); the decomposition of living organisms, and deposition from the atmosphere in dust, rain and snow. Minerals are only available to the plant when dissolved in water and even then their uptake is affected by a range of factors. These include concentration gradients between the soil solution and roots; microbiological activity within the roots, on the root surface and in the soil surrounding the roots (rhizosphere), and plant growth rate. There is increasing evidence that plants can regulate their nutrient uptake according to need, using energy to accumulate ions that they use to counteract the various levels in concentration gradients (Fitter 1997). Of course, if the water in which these minerals are dissolved is frozen, as it often is at high elevation in the mountains, these nutrients are unavailable to the plant. It is at such times that stored nutrients may be mobilized to provide an 'emergency' supply. It is also worth remembering that nutrient release into the soil solution (by weathering of rock particles and decomposition of organic detritus), as well as uptake by plant roots are, like all physico-chemical processes, affected by temperature. In the mountains, soil temperatures are generally lower during the growing season than they are in the garden, so nutrient release and uptake take place more slowly. Everything is accelerated under cultivation conditions, which causes difficulties for alpine plants that are adapted to slower rates of nutrient uptake and use. The colder the environment from which the plant originally came, the more likely this is to be a serious problem.

Phosphorus

Next to nitrogen, the element most likely to be limiting to growth in arctic-alpine ecosystems is phosphorus. Rocks typically contain much less than 1 per cent phosphorus (see section in Chapter 6 on chemical weathering) and all types of phosphate ions are extremely insoluble in combination with dominant ions in the soil, such as aluminium, iron and calcium. The availability of phosphorus is dependent on soil chemistry, and is strongly influenced by pH, since phosphorus is immobilized in either very acid or very alkaline soils.

Phosphorus
Alpine plants in soils that contain adequate nitrogen are sometimes limited in growth by a deficiency of available phosphorus. Most alpines, like their lowland counterparts, have highly evolved symbiotic relationships (known as mycorrhizas) between their roots and a range of soil fungi, enabling them to obtain sufficient phosphorus (P) in such circumstances. But at the highest elevations, on the least fertile mineral soils, the absence of the necessary fungi may limit or prevent colonization. Similarly, an absence of the appropriate mycorrhizal fungi in our gardens may also make the cultivation of some high alpines somewhat difficult, although introducing them is likely to be fraught with its own difficulties.

Primarily in order to ensure adequate phosphorus uptake under a range of difficult conditions, plants have developed another type of root symbiosis, in this case with fungi rather than bacteria. These root-fungus symbioses are known as mycorrhizas. They vary in kind, some being restricted to cells within the roots (endo-mycorrhizas) and others occurring chiefly on the root surfaces (ecto-mycorrhizas). Mycorrhizas are found, in one form or other, in most species of plants and in all habitats, although particular mycorrhizal fungi are often specific to particular plant families, genera or species. Many gardeners will be aware that members of the *Orchidaceae* and *Ericaceae* need to form effective mycorrhizas to grow optimally, or in some cases at all. Few will be aware, however, that most plants probably form mycorrhizas in nature. Logically, one might think that alpines are particularly likely to form mycorrhizas, since they are known to be particularly important for plants growing in nutrient-poor soils. However, in a recent review, Gardes and Dahlberg (1996) throw considerable doubt on this assumption. They concluded that:

1. Non-mycorrhizal plants are widespread, and predominate in certain alpine plant communities.
2. Typical endo-mycorrhizas are ubiquitous in low arctic and alpine areas, but the level of root colonization (and implied effectiveness) is highly variable.
3. Root colonization by non-pathogenic fungi that do not appear to be mycorrhizal, and whose significance is unknown, is widespread.
4. A large number of different ecto-mycorrhizal fungal types are present on a relatively few, widely distributed shrub and herbaceous plant species.
5. Ericaceous plants with ericoid mycorrhizas dominate large arctic and alpine areas covered by heath communities.

It seems that under the most extreme conditions in the Arctic, and in the mountains, mycorrhizas are rare or absent – a situation similar to that found for symbiotic nitrogen-fixing bacteria. Despite these doubts about the importance of mycorrhizas for high alpines it is possible that some species that are particularly difficult to grow in the garden are missing the presence of their normal fungal partners. Perhaps if these fungi could be introduced, and would grow and form functional mycorrhizas with the plants in question, the associated cultivation difficulties could be reduced or overcome. However, there are a number of 'ifs' here. Firstly, the mycorrhizal fungi could only be introduced to cultivation either on the roots of living plants or in soil collected from around such roots. The former is undesirable, and may be illegal on grounds of conservation, while the second risks introducing other organisms that may be pathogens. In any case it is likely that most if not all plants can be grown successfully without mycorrhizas, provided the growing medium has an appropriate composition that includes a good balance of nutrients, with adequate available phosphorus. It is also important that the pH is neither too high nor too low, around neutral (pH 7) being the optimum for most species.

Potassium, Magnesium, Calcium and Sulphur

In addition to nitrogen and phosphorus, the other essential macro-elements are potassium, magnesium, calcium and sulphur. These elements are generally obtained in sufficient quantities by alpine plants directly from the soil solution in which the roots grow, having originated from the weathering of rock-forming minerals.

Essential Micronutrients

The essential micro-elements (boron, chlorine, copper, iron, manganese, molybdenum and zinc), often referred to as trace elements, are only required by plants in very small amounts compared with the macro-elements. Nevertheless, they are equally essential for normal plant growth. These elements are generally present in adequate amounts in montane ecosystems, either in the soil by mineral weathering, or through atmospheric deposition in rain, snow and dust. However, they may not always be available to the plant, or conversely may be present in toxic amounts. The ability of particular species to cope with either extreme varies considerably, and as a result trace element deficiencies or excesses may substantially influence species distributions and plant community composition.

The best known trace element deficiency, with a major impact on the occurrence of plant species in the wild, and well known to gardeners, is that which results in leaf chlorosis (loss of chlorophyll, particularly between the veins, **Plate 7.5**), and sometimes in the death of sensitive plants growing on calcareous soils with high pH. This condition is generally known as lime-induced chlorosis, and until recently it was thought that high concentrations of calcium, particularly when associated with low levels of magnesium, were the principle cause. Acid soils (low pH) generally contain low levels of calcium and comparatively high levels of available iron and manganese. Plants growing naturally on such soils (calcifuges) have evolved to cope with these conditions, and seem to require iron and

Left: 7.5 Interveinal leaf chlorosis in *Kalmiopsis leachiana* caused by nutrient imbalance.

Lime-induced chlorosis?

The pH of soils is often critical in determining which plants will grow on them. So-called calcifuge (acid-loving) plants, such as rhododendrons and many other members of the heath family (Ericaceae), and some gentians and primulas are usually only found on acidic soils in the wild, and are unable to grow on calcareous (limey) soils of high pH in cultivation. They typically develop leaf chlorosis under such conditions, which limits growth and may result in a lingering death. Until recently it has been thought that lime (calcium carbonate) in high pH soil solutions induces chlorosis in calcifuge species; hence the term lime-induced chlorosis. It was also thought that the ratio of calcium to magnesium in the soil solution was important, and that chlorosis could be prevented or cured by the addition of magnesium.

This is now known not to be the case; it seems that high pH, which limits the availability of iron and manganese to plants, is the chief factor. This is in keeping with the knowledge that chlorosis can usually be rapidly reversed by watering the plants with a chemical solution containing sequestered iron and manganese. Rhododendrons growing healthily in alkaline soils in the Himalayas have been shown to be tolerant of high concentrations of calcium and high calcium:magnesium ratios, and it seems that this is primarily due to their ability to extract adequate iron and manganese from the soil solution and, in the case of manganese, accumulate it in their foliage. It has been suggested that once manganese has been accumulated in the leaves it is recycled when the leaves decay, providing an available pool of manganese that sustains future growth.

It has also been suggested that chlorosis on alkaline soils is caused by phosphorus deficiency, due to phosphorus becoming 'locked up' in high pH solutions (see main text on phosphorus). It has been possible to reverse chlorosis in some, but not all, calcifuges tested, by providing them with additional phosphorus.

Yet another theory suggests that differences between plant communities on acidic and calcareous soils are primarily due not to differences in soil chemistry but to differences in soil water status. Acidic soils are generally less well drained than calcareous soils and thus lay wetter, which influences soil aeration and nutrient turnover as well as water availability. Some plants are better able to withstand these conditions than others.

manganese in available forms – being unable to extract these elements from alkaline soil solutions, as calcicoles (lime-loving plants) are able to do (but see below). Hence calcifuge plants are principally found on acid soils in nature, forming the specialized plant communities of acid bogs, acid heaths and alpine habitats on acidic rock formations. If these plants are grown in alkaline soils, depending on their sensitivity they will sooner or later show symptoms of chlorosis. In cultivation, the symptoms can generally be removed easily by applying 'sequestered' ('chelated') iron (iron in a chemically bound form), uptake of which is not inhibited by calcium and high pH.

It was suggested by Tod (1971a and b), as a result of extensive tests with rhododendrons under controlled conditions, that magnesium deficiency rather than excess calcium is often, but not always, the principal cause of chlorosis in this genus. Like others at this time, Tod thought that this particular cholorosis might be due to the magnesium competing with calcium for uptake by plants. This was a reasonable assumption, given that calcium and magnesium are chemically similar, but it is now known that calcium and magnesium do not actually compete for uptake in this way.

Continuing studies by Rankin and colleagues (McAleese et al. 1999; McAleese and Rankin 2000; Rankin 2001) involve reconsideration of the question of how rhododendrons that go chlorotic when grown on calcareous soils in cultivation are able to grow healthily on limy soils in the wild, as reported by plant hunters from George Forrest onwards. Rankin's group have collected plant materials and associated rock, soil and water samples from the wild in China, and from healthy and chlorotic plants in cultivation, and then analyzed them for various minerals and pH. They first showed conclusively that the roots of healthy rhododendrons in the wild were often growing in direct contact with limestone, and bathed with highly alkaline water, rich in calcium carbonate. In such instances they sometimes found known calcicoles, such as *Daphne calcicola* and *Primula forrestii* (**Plate 7.6**), growing in close proximity to the rhododendrons. Firstly, this scotched the oft-repeated suggestions that rhododendrons growing on limestone in the wild are: (1) able to avoid chlorosis because they have their roots in an acidic humus layer, overlying the limestone, or (2) that the limestone is hard, and therefore only dissolves slowly and is carried away from the roots rapidly by monsoon rains. Secondly, they showed that in these highly alkaline soils magnesium content was low, indicating that magnesium was not an important factor.

Looking for other explanations of lime-tolerance mechanisms by rhododendrons in the wild, and reasons for their intolerance of high pH and calcium carbonate in cultivation, Rankin and co-workers turned once more to a consideration of the

importance of iron and manganese, both of which are essential micronutrients. Their tentative conclusion, backed up by limited experimental evidence, is that manganese is of key importance in the wild. They suggest that rhododendrons, and some other members of the *Ericaceae*, are able to slowly accumulate large amounts of manganese from alkaline soils that contain little, after which the manganese released from leaf litter provides a steady supply thereafter. Further research is required to verify these findings (Rankin 2001). As far as cultivated plants are concerned, Rankin's analyses of chlorotic cultivated plants show that in some cases at least either iron or manganese is at a critically low level, with manganese deficiency being more common. Application of sequestered iron is likely to cure chlorosis caused by manganese deficiency, as well as that due to iron deficiency, because commercially available sequestered iron products always contain some sequestered manganese.

Phosphorus deficiency has also been suggested as having a major role in lime-induced chlorosis. Recent studies (Tyler 1994) have shown that it is possible to grow a range of calcifuge plants (though not all that were tested) in limestone soil of pH 8, provided that the level of phosphate in the soil is increased sufficiently. At normal levels in this and similar calcareous soils the phosphorous is rendered chemically unavailable to the plants because of the high pH factor. It seems that sufficient additional phosphorus has to be added to more than overcome this phosphorus immobilizing capacity of the soil. Clearly there are several chemical

Above: 7.6 *Primula forrestii*, seen here growing among limestone rocks in Yunnan, is a known calcicole and should be grown in composts containing ground limestone for best results.

mechanisms involved in determining the ability or inability of sensitive plants to grow on high pH calcareous soils, and these vary in different species, and perhaps also in differing situations.

In another recent study Michalet *et al.* (2002) investigated the possibility that soil water status, as well as soil chemistry, might influence plant community composition and biomass. Acid soils overlying granitic rock are generally less free-draining than calcareous soils overlying limestones and base-rich pelites, and they felt that this difference in soil moisture, especially during dry periods in summer, might profoundly influence which species grow on the different soil types. As well as measuring various factors influencing soil water availability, they also measured above-ground biomass and available nitrogen and phosphorus in plots on calcareous sites overlying dolomitic limestone, and on acidic soils overlying gneissose metamorphic rocks. Species richness and above-ground biomass were highly correlated with substrate type, being greater on the calcareous soil. However, soil water status, rather than the pH of the soil or its chemistry, appeared to be the principal factor in determining these differences.

Serpentinite Soils

It has been known for many years that some species of plants, many rare or with localized distributions, are either found growing only on serpentinite (ultramafic) soils, or are more likely to be found on soils derived from serpentinite than elsewhere. This is of special interest to plant ecologists because serpentinite soils are generally toxic to plants as a result of their unique chemical and physical properties (i.e. generally high pH associated with low levels of available calcium and high levels of magnesium; low nitrogen and phosphorus content, often high trace-element levels of heavy metals including nickel, chromium, and cobalt; mercury may also be present locally; low water-holding capacity and cation exchange capacity.

Serpentinite is found in various places around the world including Mediterranean Europe, Turkey, UK (particularly the Lizard), New Caledonia, Queensland, Philippines, Brazil, Cuba, southern Africa, Pacific states and eastern states of the USA and Canada. Areas dominated by serpentinite generally occur as geological 'islands' in a sea of other soil types. Many serpentinite bodies are the relics of ancient ocean floors that have been thrust upwards during mountain building episodes. Serpentinite is associated typically with other ultramafic rocks composed mainly of olivine and pyroxene, and basalt, along with small amounts of sedimentary rocks such as chert, mudstone and limestone. In some occurrences, particularly in the European Alps, there are schists rich in the magnesium silicate mineral, talc. In warm temperate climates, woodland soils on serpentinite are developed over red-brown residual clay deposits, but at higher altitudes, soils are poorly developed or absent, with much bare rock covered in part by a thin cover of small fragments of weathered serpentinite.

When these rocks were exposed, plant species dispersed onto them from the surrounding substrates. Eventually, those that could colonize and survive on serpentinite soils evolved on a separate trajectory from their non-serpentinite relatives. In many cases the new species survived on a patch of serpentinite because they were poor competitors on other substrates – they could not 'escape' (Lyons 2001). As a result of this island effect, serpentinite substrates support a large number of species that are found only on this rock type and have restricted ranges. As an illustration of their importance for rare plants, in California serpentinite soils cover only 1% of the land surface, but host 10% of the endemic flora of the state, 282 serpentinite species being listed as rare by the California Native Plant Society. Some of these rarities are threatened due to anthropogenic causes (development, mining, damage by off-road vehicles), but many are rare simply because they are unusually restricted in their distribution. And, while they are not found in many locations, they may be locally abundant (Brooks 1987). Unlike rare species that have faced an unnatural contraction in their numbers, serpentinite endemics are rare by nature. This suggests that for many such species conservation is straightforward. Set the land aside, and as long as it remains undisturbed the plants will persist without further assistance as they have for thousands of years (Kruckeberg 1984).

Below: 7.7 *Calochortus amabilis* growing in serpentine soil. Bear Valley, California.

Not all species growing on serpentinite are restricted to these soils. Species with the ability to grow on and off serpentinite are called bodenvags, a German word meaning indifferent. This indifference allows them to be more common and widely distributed. Research suggests that bodenvags often comprise geographically close but genetically distinct populations, some of which can tolerate serpentinite, others which cannot. Such populations may be separated by only a few metres at the boundary between serpentinite and other soils.

As noted earlier, serpentinite occurs quite widely around the world, but most serpentinite endemics of interest to alpine gardeners hail from areas in western North America and the eastern Mediterranean. In the American west there are a number of genera that are particularly associated with serpentinite, although in no case are all species found only on this soil type. Among bulbs, Allium, Calochortus, Fritillaria and Lilium all contain serpentinite endemics, while among non-bulbous genera, Eriogonum, Hesperolinon, Monardella and Phacelia, to name but a few, also contain species restricted to serpentinite. Much less is known in detail about the occurrence and distribution of serpentinite endemics in the eastern Mediterranean, but genera including Alyssum, Anthemis, Arenaria, Campanula, Centaurea, Eryngium, Fritillaria, Silene and Thymus are all known to contain examples.

Adaptation to serpentinite soils is likely to involve both physiological and morphological modifications. Physiological requirements are likely to include ability to tolerate drought, nutrient deficiency and high concentrations of heavy metals. With regard to heavy metal tolerance, a few species have been shown to possess the ability to accumulate very high levels of nickel, cobalt or chromium in their leaves (hyperaccumulators) without it causing them problems; others seem to tolerate heavy metals by excluding them when taking up other elements from the soil solution. Morphological modifications include nanism (reduces water loss and mineral nutrient requirements), glaucescence (waxy cuticles reduce water loss), ground-hugging habit (similarly reduces water loss) and colour changes that confer uncertain benefits (Kruckeberg 1992).

It might be thought that serpentinite endemics would be difficult to cultivate, but in practice there is ample evidence that they respond well to normal cultivation techniques. Certainly, they generally demand especially well-drained soils which are not overburdened with available nutrients, but this is no more than is required by many alpines. If in doubt, treat a plant from serpentinite the same as you would its close relatives from normal soils and in most cases success will be yours.

8·REPRODUCTION

Successful reproduction, through which an organism passes on its genes to future generations, is the ultimate aim of all living things, and alpine plants have evolved a wide range of reproductive mechanisms. In severe environments, such as arctic and alpine habitats, abiotic (non-living) factors strongly influence plant reproduction. For example, the timing of snow disappearance significantly influences the timing of flowering for many alpine plants (Kudo 1991), while the relatively rapid flowering and fruiting of most alpine species is an adaptation to the short growing season (Bliss 1971). The resources available for the development of sexual organs (which requires a lot of energy), are reduced due to low carbon fixation during the short summer, and therefore sexual reproduction is often reduced or dispensed with. This is in spite of the fact that sexual reproduction confers potential evolutionary advantage on a population over a number of generations: the mixing of genes from different parents produces new combinations, upon which natural selection may act.

An alternative strategy, generally less energy costly than sexual reproduction but more risky in terms of long-term survival of the species, is to reproduce mainly or exclusively by vegetative propagules (that is, by clonal reproduction). In both cases, the 'cost' of reproduction can be reduced by the plant being long-lived, thus reducing the need for frequent successful reproduction in order to maintain a population. As mentioned earlier (see Chapter 3), these factors contribute to there being relatively few annuals and biennials in high alpine plant communities, compared with those from lower elevations.

Sexual and asexual reproduction
Successful reproduction is the ultimate measure of success for all living organisms. Sexual reproduction is evolutionarily advantageous for a species since it provides a range of plants with new combinations of genes, from which individuals well fitted to current environmental conditions can be selected. However, sexual reproduction is costly in terms of energy consumption and often fraught with difficulty in extreme alpine environments. Because of this, asexual reproduction often predominates in such cases.

Flower Development, Pollination and Seed Set

One of the most characteristic features of many arctic and high alpine species, uncommon in plants of less hostile environments, is the possession of pre-formed flower buds. Rather than being formed on the current year's growth, flower buds are initiated in the previous season and are ready to develop rapidly to maturity in spring. This phenomenon is particularly well developed in snowbed species because they have the shortest growing period of all alpines. Plants such as soldanellas, snowbed erythroniums and pulsatillas routinely flower within days of the snow melting or even, in the case of the soldanellas, push their precocious flowers up through the melting snow (**Plate 8.1**). In cultivation such species often flower very early in the season and may be stimulated to do so even earlier by a spell of mild weather. In a Japanese study of the snowbed species *Primula cuneifolia* ssp. *hakusanensis*, flower buds formed the previous year were found to open in late July, immediately after snowmelt, seed was set and the leaves were beginning to wither by mid-September; winter buds were formed by early October (Shibata and Nishida 1993).

While in most species that have been studied pre-formed flower buds are initiated during the previous growing season, in some species they may take several years to develop. For example, *Polygonum viviparum* is an extreme case requiring 3-4 years (Diggle 1997), while *Caltha leptosepala* (**Plate 8.2**) requires 2-3 years (Aydelotte and Diggle 1997). It is not uncommon in some species (for example, *Ranunculus glacialis*) for two or three future cohorts of flower buds, from several previous years, to be present at one time. In a particularly good alpine growing season flowers formed over several less favourable seasons may all open at once, which makes for a spectacular sight and, if good conditions continue into the period of seed set and development, a bumper seed crop.

Below left: 8.1 *Soldanella minima* pushing up through the melting snow.

Below right: 8.2 The flowers of the snowbed species *Caltha leptosepala* are pre-formed 2-3 years before they open.

The repeated independent evolution of flower pre-formation, which is found in all high mountains and among unrelated plant families, suggests that pre-formed flowers confer a considerable reproductive advantage on plants growing in cold environments. Unfortunately, flowers formed on snowbed alpines in the autumn are vulnerable when the plants are grown in snow-free lowland gardens. Being precocious they are prone to damage by the freeze-thaw of lowland winters; they are also vulnerable to attack by molluscs and other pests that remain active during mild spells in winter. Soldanellas are a case in point, and it is by no means unusual for a plant to be completely stripped of its dormant flower buds by a combination of slugs, snails and freeze-thaw during the winter.

Pre-formed flower buds
Pre-formed flower buds, which usually open in the season after that in which they were initiated, are much more common in alpine plants than in those from other habitats. This is an adaptation to enable the plants to flower as soon as the conditions are right in spring, so that they have the whole of a short growing season in which to set and ripen their seeds. Pre-formed flower buds are particularly common in snowbed species, the classic case being soldanellas, which often flower through the melting snow.

Despite the frequency of pre-formed flowers in high alpines not all, or even most, alpine plant species develop them; it is likely that more than half only flower after the annual crop of leaves has been fully developed (Körner 1999). Whereas pre-formed flowers are stimulated to develop and open principally by increasing temperature, those which mature once the foliage is developed are probably influenced more by day length. In some species increasing day length provides the stimulus (in early flowerers, such as the primulas, ranunculi and saxifrages), in others decreasing day length after midsummer triggers flowering (in late flowerers, such as many campanulas and members of the daisy family). Some genera (notably, as far as alpine gardeners are concerned, *Gentiana*) have both late- and early-flowering species.

The question arises as to why there is so much variation in time of flowering of arctic and alpine plants, despite the very short growing season. The answer may be that early- and late-flowering plants have different life history strategies (the pattern of development, reproduction and dying). Based on a study of 137 species, in northern Sweden, Molau (1993) proposed that early-flowering species set relatively few fertile seeds, but that those seeds or fruits that are set have a very high chance of maturing. By contrast, late-flowering species set more seed, but have a lower chance of maturing them before winter returns. In a similar study in alpine fellfields in Japan, but in this case restricted to 10 ericaceous species, Kudo and Suzuki (2002) found that here, too, late-flowering species tended to set more fruit than those flowering earlier in the season. By excluding pollinating insects they showed that this difference was largely due to variations in pollen availability, associated with varying insect activity; later in the season the higher air temperatures stimulate more insect activity and hence greater pollen transfer.

Complementary to this variation in seeding success is a variation in the breeding system. There is a greater incidence of cross-pollination rather than self-pollination in early-flowering species, and a higher frequency of self-pollination, apomixis (seed development without pollination) and vivipary (development of unpollinated ovules into bulbils or mini-plantlets in the seed head) in late-flowering species. It should be noted in relation to what follows that as apomixis and vivipary do not involve fertilization of the ovule, the offspring are genetically identical to the parent.

Apomixis and vivipary

Apomixis (seed development without pollination) and vivipary (development of unpollinated ovules into bulbils or miniature plantlets in the seed head) occur more frequently in alpine plants that in those of most other habitats. These mechanisms generally bring an enhanced probability of successful reproduction, but the resultant plants are clones of their parents and hence do not contribute to the distribution of new combinations of genes upon which natural selection can work. Alpines that have a wide altitudinal range and the capability for asexual reproduction, such as *Polygonum viviparum*, generally show a decline in seed set, and an increasing incidence of asexual reproduction, with increasing elevation. Plants that employ occasional sexual reproduction by fertilized seeds (the norm in other plants) and frequent reproduction by apomixis can give rise to taxonomic confusion. This is because each of the differing individuals produced by sexual reproduction can be multiplied up by repeated apomixes, giving the appearance of a very variable species, with a range of apparently stable forms that are effectively clones. Hawkweeds (*Hieracium* spp.) and dandelions (*Taraxacum* spp.) are classic examples.

Increased frequency of apomixis and vivipary with increasing altitude is characteristic of alpine plants, probably because pollination is often unreliable in hostile environments with few pollinating insects, and normal seed production by pollination of an ovule is energy-costly. A large excess of energy-rich ovules and pollen grains has to be produced in order to ensure a reasonable chance of successful pollination, most of which are then wasted. Apomixis and vivipary are much less wasteful of energy, as is vegetative reproduction, which also increases in importance with altitude. Many arctic-alpine plants exhibit apparently normal seed production, but some or all of the seeds are produced apomictically (without fertilization). Some species are obligate apomicts, so that all their seeds are always produced in this way, as for instance in the genera *Alchemilla* and *Antennaria*. The more common condition, however, is facultative apomixis, in which the seeds may be formed either by the normal sexual process or, in more severe environmental conditions or where pollinators are lacking, without fertilization. This is found in the genera *Ranunculus* and *Polygonum*, among many others. More commonly, facultative apomixis is characterized by predominantly asexual reproduction, alternating with occasional sexual reproduction. This can lead to an immense variability in morphology within the species, because each of the offspring resulting from sexual fertilization can subsequently reproduce for many generations apomictically, giving rise to large populations of apparently stable types which are effectively clones. This is typical of, among others, the grass genus *Poa*, the genera *Hieracium* (hawkweeds) and *Taraxacum* (dandelions), in the Asteraceae, and can lead to the erroneous conclusion that the different types are actually separate species or sub-species.

The fact that sexual seed reproduction occurs at all in difficult environments, where energy and pollinators are in short supply, is testament to the considerable evolutionary advantages of the recombination of genes it achieves. This is optimized in cross-fertilization between different individuals. Many studies have shown that inbreeding associated with self-pollination reduces reproductive success and 'fitness' of offspring. For example, Montalvo (1994) showed that in *Aquilegia caerulea* self-pollinated flowers produced fewer seeds than cross-pollinated flowers. Also, seedlings grown from seeds of self-pollinated flowers were smaller at all stages of growth to maturity than seedlings grown from seeds of cross-pollinated flowers, and hence were less likely to breed successfully. Nevertheless, self-pollination may be the main means by which insect-pollinated (entomophilous) plants reproduce in the most extreme arctic and alpine environments because strong winds and short growing periods reduce pollinator activity and thus reduce the opportunity for cross-pollination.

Cross-fertilization and self-fertilization

Cross-fertilization between flowers of different individuals is more successful in producing viable seed than self-fertilization, and the resultant plants are generally larger and likely to reach flowering size more quickly. Nevertheless, in high alpine environments where insect pollinators are few and environmental conditions often prevent them from flying, self-fertilization is often more common. This being so, the fact that many alpines allocate considerable resources to the production of large and/or numerous flowers as insect-attractors emphasizes the considerable evolutionary advantage of even occasional cross-fertilization.

Top left: 8.3 *Gentiana occidentalis* has large, showy flowers to attract pollinating insects.

Top right: 8.4 The large flowers of *Geum reptans* show up well against the dark background of the foliage and rocks in which the plant grows, making them easy to see by pollinating insects.

Bottom: 8.5 *Androsace alpina* provides an attractive floral display for visiting pollinators by virtue of a high concentration of individually small flowers.

Middle left: 8.6 Fly visiting a flower of *Merendera montana*. Picos de Europa.

So advantageous is sexual reproduction that many entomophilous alpines devote huge resources to facilitating it. Flowers of high alpines are generally large, as in trumpet gentians (**Plate 8.3**), campanulas, ranunculi and *Geum reptans* (**Plate 8.4**). Or they are numerous and grouped together, so as to produce a comparable floral display, as in androsaces (**Plate 8.5**), saxifrages and cushion phloxes. Whereas leaf size generally decreases in the species within a genus at increasing elevations in which the species occur, flower size or number does not. Not only do these large or numerous flowers of insect-pollinated high alpines cost a great deal of energy to produce but, by shading the leaves, they also reduce the energy available for photosynthesis. Taken together these factors may result in as much as 40 per cent of the season's photosynthetic carbon gain being allocated to flower production; a much higher proportion than for equivalent lowland species. Such extravagant allocation of resources to flower production is necessary because there is a limited variety and abundance of suitable pollinating insects at high elevations and latitudes (**Plate 8.6**). In order to be noticed by insects, the floral display must be greater. Many authors have reported that pollinators visit large floral displays more frequently than small ones (for example, Heinrich 1979, Ohara and Higashi 1994), while also visiting more flowers on larger displays (Geber 1985, Harder and Barrett 1995).

It is worth noting that very different reproductive strategies may on occasion be found even between co-occurring species of the same genus. Thus Philipp et al. (1996) found that each of four *Pedicularis* species growing at a site in arctic Greenland had different strategies, even though they all had similar flowers,

adapted for insect pollination: *Pedicularis lanata* was shown to depend on insects for seed set; *P. hirsuta* and *P. flammea* were able to set viable seed by self-pollination, and *P. lapponica* mainly propagated itself vegetatively, rarely setting seed. The fact that all four species can co-exist for prolonged periods suggests that each of these reproductive strategies is successful, although the relative success of each is likely to vary spatially and temporally, in response to varying environmental conditions.

Pollination in arctic and alpine plants other than grasses, which are almost always wind-pollinated, is predominantly by insects. In the Caucasus, 89 per cent of non-graminaceous (non-grass) flowering plants were shown to be insect pollinated, the remainder being pollinated by wind. A few species rely on more exotic pollinators: thus *Penstemon newberryi* and *P. davidsonii* have both been shown to be pollinated by hummingbirds in the Sierra Nevada of California, while these wondrous birds also pollinate the metre-high (3-foot) *Lupinus alopecuroides* in the Andes. It seems that long-tongued insects such as moths and butterflies can act as surrogate pollinators, at least for the penstemons, since both set good seed in areas far removed from the haunts of hummingbirds.

Pollination

Alpines are mostly insect-pollinated, principally by short-tongued bees, bumblebees, flies, butterflies and moths. Although bumblebees only fly at air temperatures above 10°C (50°F) they have been found visiting flowers at up to 5,100 metres (16,700 feet) in the Hindu Kush. Flies operate at lower temperatures and in dimmer light than bees or butterflies and are found at even higher elevations, generally pollinating flat, open flowers, for example many Apiaceae, Asteraceae, Brassicaceae and Rosaceae. Long-tubed flowers (many Lamiaceae, Orchidaceae, Primulaceae and Scrophulariaceae) are generally pollinated by bumblebees, butterflies or moths.

The principal kinds of pollinating insects for plants in the high mountains are short-tongued bees, bumblebees (syn. humblebees, Hymenoptera), flies (Diptera), butterflies and moths (Lepidoptera). However, where ants are common and other insects are relatively scarce, ants may be important pollinators. Thus a study in the Spanish Sierra Nevada by Gómez *et al.* (1996) showed that 70-100 per cent of the flower visitors to three alpine plant species (*Arenaria tetraquetra*, *Alyssum purpureum* and *Sedum anglicum*) were ants. In another study in New South Wales, Australia, Ramsey (1995) found that the perennial herb *Blandfordia grandiflora* was self-pollinated by ants and that this resulted in increased seed set compared with unassisted self-pollination.

Bumblebees are, perhaps surprisingly given their energy-demanding flight, more common at high altitude in the mountains of the Northern Hemisphere than any other kinds of bees. In many places they are the only bees present. They fly only during the day when air temperature is above 10°C (50°F). Under favourable conditions they have been found at up to 5,100 metres (16,700 feet) in the Hindu Kush where they were pollinating, among other genera, *Oxytropis*, *Astragalus* and *Hedysarum*. Flies can work at lower temperatures and in dimmer light than bees or butterflies. Long-tubed flowers are usually pollinated by bumblebees or lepidoptera while small, flat flowers, for example Brassicaceae (Cruciferae) and Rosaceae, are mostly pollinated by flies.

Seed set and maturation

Successful pollination and subsequent development of the seed to maturity require a lot of energy. Flowers that trap energy are therefore at an advantage, particularly in cold environments. Large flowers trap more solar energy than small ones, and if they are shaped parabolically, like a satellite dish, they focus that energy onto the centre of the flower, where the reproductive organs are located. This not only aids pollination and seed development directly, but also attracts more insects, which come to bask in the sun. Some species with parabolic flowers go a stage further, following the sun as it moves across the sky and thereby maximizing energy gain (heliotropism). An alternative strategy for keeping floral organs and developing seeds warm is to envelop them in insulating down.

The reason for the puzzling predominance of white flowers in the New Zealand flora has been the subject of much debate. Godley (1979) has noted that 61 per cent of the New Zealand flora is white, compared with 25 per cent of the British flora. But an even greater proportion of New Zealand mountain flowers are white: 78 per cent compared with only 37 per cent for the coastal lowlands. Mark and Adams (1973) suggested that this predominance of white flowers might be due to the kinds of insect pollinators that predominate in the New Zealand mountains. Richards (1995) reviewed the evidence and concluded that this was indeed the case. New Zealand alpine flowers are typically bowl-shaped, and being white they reflect the sun's rays into the centre of the flower, forming a warm spot that is attractive to insects, especially flies. Specialized pollinating insects, which are typically attracted by bright colours, are either lacking (long-tongued bees) or scarce (butterflies) in the New Zealand fauna, especially in the mountains. Thus insect pollination appears to be carried out largely and quite efficiently by flies, with beetles, moths and short-tongued bees playing smaller roles.

Where there is a greater range of flower colour among the flora there may be characteristic seasonal changes in the dominant colours. For instance Ram *et al.* (1988) noted that in the central Himalayas, the season starts mainly with blue and pink (*Gentiana, Primula*), changes to yellow (*Ranunculus, Taraxacum*), and then white at early peak season (*Anemone*), merging into a mix of yellow and red when the monsoon season begins in July (*Polygonum, Potentilla, Geum*). In August, red and blue take over (*Polygonum, Cyananthus*) followed by white in September (*Selenium, Anaphalis*), the season closing with blue again (*Gentiana, Cyananthus*). It is likely that such flower colour periodicity is associated with insect pollinator preferences, but this has not yet been researched and it may simply reflect the dominance of certain genera at certain times. In the Alps there is not such a clear periodicity of flower colour, although there is a strong tendency for white flowers, especially Ranunculus, to predominate early in the season in the higher meadows, to be replaced later by yellows (*Leontodon, Hieracium, and Rhinanthus*).

An intriguing characteristic of the flowers of some arctic and alpine plants, which they share with the very un-alpine sunflower, is 'sun tracking' (heliotropism). Species such as *Dryas octopetala, Hymenoxis grandiflora* (**Plate 8.7**) and *Ranunculus glacialis* keep their flowers facing the sun. Heliotropism, together with the

Below: 8.7 Sun tracking is common among alpine plants but is especially obvious in members of the *Asteraceae,* such as *Hymenoxys grandiflora.*

parabolic shape of their flowers, enables them to maximize the energy they capture from the sun, and reflect it towards the centre of the flower. This has a dual effect: it creates a warm spot attractive to pollinators, and may increase both the likelihood of successful pollination and the rates of growth and maturation of the seed (Crawford 1989). In a recent study in the Grossglockner region of Austria, Luzar and Gottsberger (2001) investigated heliotropism and its effects on floral biology in *Ranunculus montanus*, *R. alpestris*, *Pulsatilla alpina*, *Callianthemum coriandrifolium* (all Ranunuculaceae), and *Leucanthemopsis alpina* (Asteraceae), all of which have bowl and disc flowers (or inflorescences – clusters of flowers) that are heliotropic during periods of direct solar radiation. Air temperatures inside the flowers were above those of the ambient air for all five species. The maxima of excess temperature were between 2°C (3.6°F), in *C. coriandrifolium*, and 6.2°C (11.2°F), in *P. alpina*. In an experimental manipulation, flowers of *Ranunculus montanus* were either allowed to turn with the sun or were held in position facing north. Comparative temperature measurements showed that during sunny or slightly cloudy periods the air within the flowers having uninhibited heliotropic movements was, on average, 0.7°C (1.3°F), and in individual cases up to 1.3°C (2.3°F). This was warmer than in flowers that had been fixed to face north. For *R. montanus*, which is self-incompatible (requires cross-pollination for viable seed set), heliotropism affected the frequency and duration of visits by pollinating insects: unimpeded heliotropic flowers were visited more often, and for longer, than those flowers that had been held in position away from the sun.

There is increasing evidence that the Arctic forms of arctic-alpine species usually have the largest flowers, but more information is needed, over a wider range of species, to confirm this. If large flowers prove to be the rule for Arctic ecotypes it may well be because large flowers have the best chance of trapping as much as possible of the available sunlight energy, thereby enhancing their chances of attracting pollinators and setting viable seed during the period of long summer days.

There are other ways in which high alpines make the most of the available energy from sunlight to enhance successful sexual reproduction. Some species of *Silene* (e.g. *S. furcata* from the Arctic and *S. Antarctica*, at the other end of the world) have evolved inflated, thin-walled calyces; these act as mini-glasshouses, to aid seed ripening in the centrally placed ovary. The provision of insulation is another means of flower warming seen in many alpine genera, including *Saussurea*, *Salix* and *Eriophorum* (cotton grasses). Krog (1955) measured temperatures inside fluffy Arctic willow catkins and found them between 15°C (59°F) and 25°C (77°F) higher than ambient temperatures, when external air temperatures were

near freezing point (**Plate 8.8**). Clipping the pubescence surrounding the catkin reduced the warming effect by half. Kevan (1990) found that temperature elevation was greater and sustained for a longer period in female than in male Arctic willow catkins, and he suggested that this reflected the greater energy needs for seed set and development compared with pollen production and ripening.

Above: 8.8 The fluffy down surrounding the tiny seeds of dwarf willows provides important insulation from cold and drought.

Seed Predation

Once seed has been set and developed, the potential for successful reproduction has been achieved. However, there are a number of pitfalls to be avoided before a cohort of flourishing seedlings is in place, carrying their parents' genes into the next generation. Seeds are highly nutritious, being packed with energy intended to sustain the young seedlings while they develop their own photosynthetic apparatus sufficiently to become self-supporting. This makes seeds a very attractive food source to a wide range of organisms, including fungi and bacteria, insects and other invertebrates and, in the case of larger seeds, birds and small mammals. In addition to specialist seed feeders (such as the larvae of a wide range of beetles and seed-eating birds), there are many organisms that simply feed on seeds when the opportunity arises, or ingest them along with other edible material. Larger herbivores that graze alpine meadows may well remove most of the seed produced; the yaks that graze to high elevations in the Himalayas in summer are renowned for this, to the infuriation of everyone who tries to collect seed there.

Seed predation

Losses of seed between seed set and dispersal can be considerable. Seeds are energy packed, and therefore a very attractive food source to a wide range of organisms, including fungi and bacteria, insects and other invertebrates and, in the case of larger seeds, birds and small mammals. As well as specialist seed feeders, such as the larvae of a wide range of beetles and seed-eating birds, there are many organisms that will feed on seeds when the opportunity arises, or ingest them along with other edible material, rather than seeking them out. Larger herbivores grazing alpine meadows may well remove most of the seed produced.

In a study of factors affecting the distribution of alpine sky pilot (*Polemonium viscosum*) in lightly grazed high tundra and more heavily grazed lower krummholz habitats in Colorado, Galen (1990) found that grazed plants suffered complete loss of seed production in the current year and up to 80 per cent loss of net seed production over a three-year period. Unlike sub-alpine plants, the plants showed no capacity to compensate for losses in reproductive capacity due to grazing by producing new flowering shoots in the current season (Paige and Whitham 1987). This is perhaps surprising, since evidence indicates that such compensation can significantly reduce the reproductive cost of herbivory (Crawley 1983). A possible partial explanation is that plants such as *Polemonium viscosum* already have a genetically controlled commitment to pre-formation of flower buds for the following season, so there is no spare energy available for compensatory flower production in the current season. Removal by grazing animals of the pre-formed flower buds intended for next season would explain the carry-over effect of grazing, to the following year – noted by Galen (1990).

Seed predation is, as one might expect, highly variable in space and time, as well as being very dependent on the attractiveness of the seed (or the fruit in which seed are borne) to particular predators, and the availability of those predators at the time of seed ripening and dispersal. Thus, in a detailed study of the predation of seeds of *Sisyrinchium arenarium* (**Plate 8.9**) at two elevations in the

Below: 8.9 Seed predation of *Sisyrinchium arenarium* varied when studied at low and high elevation sites in the central Chilean Andes.

central Chilean Andes, Muñoz and Arroyo (2002) found that seed removal by ants and seed-eating birds was low at both sites (2-14 per cent), but was greater at the higher elevation of 2,700 metres (8,860 feet), where ants were the chief seed predators. Rodents, the major seed predators in shrublands at lower elevations in the same mountains, are largely absent at the higher elevations and had a negligible impact.

Seed Dispersal, Dormancy and Germination

Alpine plants have several different seed dispersal strategies, with a major division between those plants that disperse their seed over long distances and those that don't. The seeds of the former are generally identifiable by having aids to dispersal, whether by wind (most common) or animals. Parachutes, such as those found most typically in the Asteraceae, are the most effective aids for wind dispersal, but wings are a common alternative (for example, Brassicaceae and Scrophulariaceae). Studies in which these dispersal aids were removed from some seeds, and left on others, have shown that they increase dispersal distance by two to three times. Several detailed studies in the field have shown that when long-distance dispersal is involved, these aids confer considerable advantages. In a study of long-distance seed rain, over 95 days of the fruiting season of high elevation vegetation adjacent to a Swiss glacier, Stöcklin and Bäumler (1996) set out sticky traps to capture seeds and found that most seeds caught had wind-dispersion aids. Of these, 65 per cent had parachutes, 30 per cent had wings and only 5 per cent had no such aids. The latter were extremely small seeds (notably saxifrages). Over short dispersal distances of less than a metre (3 feet), seeds without dispersion aids were at much less of a disadvantage. In a similar study, but of just one unaided species (*Ranunculus adoneus*) in the Rocky Mountains, Scherf *et al*. (1994) found that virtually all the seeds remained within 16 cm (6½ in) of the maternal parent. Secondary dispersal, by being blown over a snow surface ('snow gliding') or being carried by snowmelt water or rain water, added on average 10 cm (4 in) to the primary (down slope) dispersal distance. But this is an average distance, and some seeds will always be carried much farther away from their maternal parent, perhaps to start new colonies.

It is interesting to note that in all the major studies of seed dispersal among alpine plant communities the relative proportions of seeds of different species trapped do not reflect the proportions of those species in the vegetation. This is mainly because long-lived species that reproduce primarily by vegetative means are generally grossly under-represented, while shorter-lived species that set seed freely contribute more than their share.

Seed dispersal

There are two principal seed dispersal strategies: long-distance dispersal and short-distance dispersal.

Long-distance dispersal is generally by wind, and often involves the provision of aids such as wings or parachutes. Fruits or seeds that are attractive food items to animals may be dispersed over wide areas in dung, or be carried away to a nest, as in the case of ants. Other fruits bear hooks, or other means of attaching to fur or feathers, and so get carried far and wide. Many primary colonizers have evolved long-range dispersal mechanisms to enable their seeds to be distributed from one patch of disturbed habitat to another, across unsuitable intermediate vegetation.

Short-range dispersal often simply involves the seeds falling from the seedhead. Many crevice plants and snowbed plants have evolved this mechanism, increasing the likelihood of seeds finding suitable spots to germinate in specialized niches nearby. On sheer rock faces and overhangs, spiders' webs may play an important role in trapping falling seed, which may then be drawn into crevices by the spiders when dealing with ensnared prey, or by the contraction of the net as it deteriorates and breaks up (Richards, personal communication).

While wind is the commonest agent for seed dispersal by alpine plants, animal dispersal is also important. Not all seeds consumed by seed eaters die – some is dropped before being eaten or is buried and subsequently lost or abandoned, while some germinates after passing through the guts of the animal. Indeed the seeds of many species germinate better if eaten, notably those with large, brightly coloured fruits (such as daphnes and many ericaceous shrubs) that are particularly attractive to predators. Seeds may be widely dispersed if eaten by birds or wide-ranging mammals, but few alpines depend on having hooked or sticky fruits or seeds for dispersal, unlike plants at lower elevations, where passing mammals or birds provide a more frequent and dependable means of transport.

> **Seed banks**
> The viable seed that does not germinate immediately, get eaten or die of other causes, constitutes the dormant seed bank. Seed banks are usually principally in the soil, but substantial examples may also be held amongst dense vegetation. They are particularly important in habitats exposed to frequent disturbance, and may provide the main source of seeds following avalanche, landslip or damage by skiing developments, which sweep away the pre-existing vegetation. Many factors may determine whether seeds in the soil seed bank germinate, and if the seedlings will survive to maturity.

Alpine Seed Banks

The viable seed that does not germinate immediately, get eaten, or die of other causes, constitutes the dormant seed bank. Seed banks are usually principally in the soil, but substantial examples may also be held among dense vegetation. For example, seed from cushion plants often falls between the rosettes and may remain there for many years, only germinating when the cushion dies and decays. As would be expected, dormant soil seed banks strongly reflect seed rain composition, and are therefore unreliably representative of the vegetation above them. Nevertheless, seed banks are particularly important in determining the future plant communities of habitats exposed to frequent disturbance, as most alpine habitats are. They may provide the only or principal source of the first propagules to develop following avalanche, landslip or damage by skiing developments, all of which sweep away the pre-existing vegetation (**Plate 8.10**). However, this is only the case when the damage is superficial because most dormant seeds (>75 per cent) are in the top 2 cm (¾ in) of soil. A wide range of factors may determine when, or indeed if, seeds in the soil seed bank germinate, and whether the resulting seedlings manage to survive to maturity. So it is very difficult, often impossible, to determine the significance of the soil seed bank in driving the future process of succession as far as species composition and the relevant abundance of individual species are concerned.

Above: 8.10 Ski developments can cause extensive damage to alpine plant communities, recovery being partially dependent on buried seed banks. Italian Alps.

Seed Dormancy and Germination

The mysteries surrounding seed dormancy and germination hold a special interest for keen alpine gardeners, since most of us raise many or most of our plants from seed. This reflects the fact that in alpine gardening, unlike most branches of horticulture, most plants grown are species, rather than garden hybrids or selected cultivars. Because of this, plants can be raised from seed with a reasonable expectation that they will come true to type, and this is especially so for seed collected in the wild. This is one reason why wild seed is so popular when offered in the seed exchanges, another being that many exciting species that are new to cultivation, or are re-introduced after a long absence, are only initially available this way rather than as seedlings.

Seed dormancy and germination

Seed dormancy and germination may be controlled by a range of physical, chemical and biological factors, and much remains to be determined about their relative importance in different species. The principal physical impediments to germination include hard or impermeable seed coats. Chemical factors include the presence of germination inhibitors in the seed coat or embryo (subject to alteration with time and seed exposure conditions) and the absence of growth promoters, which trigger the biochemical processes in the seed that lead to germination. The balance between inhibitors and promoters often determines whether germination takes place, and the treatments gardeners apply to encourage germination – imbibition, washing the seed to remove inhibitors, chilling or warm temperature treatments (or a combination of both), application of gibberellins (growth-promoting hormones), exposure to light or its exclusion – are designed to tip the balance in favour of germination promoters. We now know that the seeds of fewer alpines are responsive to chilling than used to be thought, and that alternating warm and cold treatments is often more effective.

Seed of many alpines shows variable germination, with seeds appearing over several seasons. This is an adaptation to severe environments, where conditions for seedling establishment may be poor in some seasons.

There is still a lot to learn about the mysteries of the physiological mechanisms that control seed dormancy and germination in alpine plants. There has been little research on alpines, compared with more popular and commercially important plants such as vegetables and annual flowers. Amateurs experimenting at home, and reporting their results through the AGS *Bulletin* and similar, have made important (if limited) contributions to knowledge of factors influencing seed dormancy and germination. In the mid-1970s I attempted to summarize the information available at the time in a series of articles in the *Bulletin* (Good 1974-75). At around the same time, unbeknown to me, a chemist at the Pennsylvania State University, Professor Norman Deno, was beginning an epic 20-year programme of research, culminating in the publication of his book, *Seed Germination Theory and Practice* (first edition Deno 1991, second edition Deno 1993) and its two supplements (Deno 1996, 1998). These three volumes provide guidance on the germination requirements of >8,000 species, many of which are alpines. The books are of particular value because Professor Deno has presented the information in a systematic way, condensing a huge research database into a limited range of simple but effective, scientifically-based pre-germination treatments, which can be practised by amateurs without the need for special equipment or expertise. For anyone seriously interested in achieving the best rates of germination from the seed that they sow, these publications are of great value.

The research done by Professor Deno, and others, shows that seed germination in arctic and alpine plants does not commonly require cold temperatures (near or below freezing point) to be triggered, contrary to what one might intuitively expect (and has often been written). Seed may often germinate slowly and unevenly in cultivation, and too often this has been assumed to be due to the absence of adequate exposure to cold temperatures. Where dormancy does occur (that is, when the seed will not germinate with warmth and moisture – and light where required), it is in fact due usually to seed-coat inhibition. The constraint may be physical (for example, prevention of water uptake by impervious seed coats), or more commonly chemical, as a result of germination inhibitors in the seed coat. In some cases there are also germination inhibitors in the embryo. In nature, hard seed coats are broken down by microbial action (sometimes in the guts of animals) and exposure to the elements, while chemical germination inhibitors are lost by gradual chemical breakdown and natural leaching processes. In cultivation, physical seed-coat inhibition can generally be overcome by scarification. This might involve shaking, stirring, or in more recalcitrant cases gently grinding, the seed with sand. Sufficiently large seed-coats can be individually ground with sandpaper. Chemical scarification using strong acids may be appropriate for large seeds with very hard seed coats, but is rarely necessary and must be done with care. Chemical germination inhibitors in the seed coat may generally be removed by soaking the seed in water, perhaps with the addition of a surfactant (washing-up liquid works well) to improve penetration. Running water is sometimes said to be more effective as there is a greater diffusion gradient for the inhibitor(s) between the seed coat and the eluent (solvent) solution. Also, running water contains more oxygen than still water: this may both aid the breakdown of the inhibitor(s) in the seed coat and aid other processes in the seed that lead to germination.

It appears that germination of alpine seeds in nature is controlled mainly through environmental, rather than physiological factors. Normally, germination cannot take place before winter, since seed usually matures too late in the season to find the right conditions of temperature and moisture over sufficient time. Optimum temperatures for germination are sufficiently high, at 20-30°C (68-86°F) in most tested alpine species, to ensure this. The most effective temperature regime for germination generally involves substantial diurnal temperature fluctuation – constant high temperatures are not as effective as high daytime temperatures alternating with much lower night-time temperatures. In the wild, most germination generally takes place soon after snowmelt begins; as soon as daytime temperatures are high enough. In many species, however, some of the seeds will not germinate in the first season, nor even perhaps in the second. This indicates variable degrees of dormancy within seedlots, not necessarily related to chilling requirements. As an adaptive mechanism, this ensures that germination is spread over several seasons and reduces the chance of complete failure that might occur if all the seedlings appeared in what turned out to be a particularly hostile season.

Staggered germination of this kind is often retained in cultivation, indicating a physiological control mechanism. For example, in a study of the germination of snow tussock grass (*Chionochloa rigida*) seed obtained from the New Zealand mountains, Mark (1965) found that at 21°C (70°F), in the dark, only 31 per cent had germinated after 50 days; 40 per cent after 109 days, and the last germination did not occur until almost 4 years later, at which time 94 per cent of the seed had germinated. Clearly, in the case of rare or particularly desirable species, there is something in the old adage that one should keep seed pans for at least three years, to maximize the number of seedlings produced. But this is only worthwhile if you can keep the seed pans weeded and watered, and in a suitable partly shaded location throughout this period.

While the seeds of most high alpines do not require chilling to germinate, many seem to benefit from a period of storage (at any temperature significantly colder than the optimum temperature for germination). During this period, germination inhibitors in the seed may break down and essential maturation processes take place. Perhaps surprisingly, on first consideration, seeds of species from lower elevations often respond to low temperatures more than alpines do. These low temperature-responders include many species that we include in our catholic definition of 'alpines', as far as the garden is concerned. In their case, a chilling requirement is a defence against germination in autumn – when conditions may be satisfactory, but the chances of the resultant seedlings surviving the winter will be low. In cultivation, provided it is sown at a time when several weeks of cold (not necessarily freezing) weather can be expected, the seed is likely to receive the necessary chilling to ensure good germination. There is no harm (and may be some benefit in certain cases) in the long-established practice among alpine gardeners, of exposing ungerminated pans of seed to cold temperatures; few seeds will be harmed and some may be stimulated to germinate that would not otherwise do so. An alternative is to pre-chill the seed in a refrigerator before sowing. The seed should be moist throughout the chilling period, since research shows (Chambers *et al.* 1990; Körner 1999) that seeds chilled when moist germinate much faster than those chilled when dry. For example, when seeds of *Geum rossii* were stored wet and cold at 4°C (40°F) for 90 days before being sown in an 18/4°C (64/40°F) day/night temperature regime, 50 per cent germinated after 5 days – compared with 16 days when the seed was stored dry and cold. Similar differences were found for seven other alpine species and in no case did seeds given a cold period when dry germinate faster than those given the same cold period but kept moist.

Seed of most alpine plants that have been tested will germinate satisfactorily in darkness, or at least in the reduced daylight that percolates through a fine covering of soil, scree material or grit covering used for pots. There are some genera however, notably *Gentiana* and *Primula*, with a number of species that require exposure to light to trigger germination. For more information, see the list in my article in the September 1975 issue of the AGS *Bulletin* (Good 1974-5). It is therefore sensible when planting seed of these genera either to sow it on the surface of the compost or to apply only a very light covering.

Seedling Establishment

Little is known about seedling establishment in the wild in the mountains because it is very difficult to observe. However, in a recent study in the Austrian Alps, Schlag and Erschbaumer (2000) observed seedling recruitment and establishment on two moraines adjacent to a glacier that had been ice-free for 25 years and 40 years respectively. Comparisons were made between vegetated and bare-ground areas on each moraine over three growing seasons.

Seedling establishment
Little is known about seedling establishment of alpines in the wild because it is difficult to study individual seedlings regularly, and for a prolonged period, given the extreme climate and generally difficult terrain. However, it is likely that establishment is the most critical stage in the life of any alpine seedling, and that the success rate is generally very low – often zero. Establishing an effective root system early, to both anchor the plant and allow it access to water and essential nutrients, is of key importance, and particularly so in unstable habitats such as scree.

On half of the plots of each type, seeds of moraine species were sown and their germination rates tracked. Wide annual fluctuations in seedling recruitment were noted over the three years of the study. Overall, however, there were no significant differences in the numbers of seedlings recruited in the different treatments. Species composition of the seedlings reflected the vegetation of the sites, and seedling recruitment was greater in the vegetated areas than on bare ground: established plants and stones represented safe sites for seedling recruitment. On the older (40 year-old), but not on the younger (25 year-old) moraine, established plants had a negative effect on the survival of seedlings. After two winters, seedling survival rates on the differing plots ranged from 0 to 40 per cent. Greater numbers of seedlings were found on the seeded than on the unseeded plots in most cases, but the advantage of sowing seed (rather than relying on natural dispersal in the 'un-sown' plots) was not significant. It is worth noting that the seeding experiment also showed that seeds of species that naturally colonize late in the successional process were able to become established on younger moraines. This suggests that it might be their relative immobility rather than any inherent inability to germinate on early successional sites that generally limits their involvement in the early stages of succession.

Having germinated and started to establish itself in a hostile environment, the seedling is first likely to devote most of what energy it has to root production; shoot production generally comes a little later, but cannot be delayed too long because the plant must begin to photosynthesize if it is to survive. This natural tendency of the alpine seedling to produce roots rather than shoots explains the surprisingly large root systems of tiny seedlings in our seed pans. It suggests that it is a good idea to sow the seed thinly, and prick out the seedlings as soon as possible. That way they will be able to make all the root growth they can, without having to compete for water and nutrients. Also, the risk of much of the root system being lost, as often occurs when seed is sown thickly and pricking out is delayed, will be eliminated. What is more, the best way to get seedlings through the difficult establishment period is to keep them growing as fast as possible, under the best possible growing conditions.

Vegetative (Clonal) Reproduction

Despite the evolutionary advantages of sexual reproduction, increase by vegetative propagation is often the main means of reproduction in arctic-alpine plants. This is at least true in terms of ground cover and biomass production, if not in terms of the number of species using the method. The relative importance of vegetative multiplication in alpines generally increases with elevation (Bliss 1971, Billings 1974). Some individual alpine plant species exemplify this changeover, reproducing solely or largely by seed at lower elevations, but mainly by vegetative means at higher elevations. This reflects decreasing availability of energy with increasing elevation, alongside decreasing likelihood of successful seed set and maturation. For example, *Oxyria digyna* (mountain sorrel), a widespread arctic-alpine species, is non-rhizomatous, and reproduces by seed in the central Rocky Mountains. But populations from harsher environments in northern Alaska reproduce mainly by rhizomes. Similarly in *Polygonum viviparum*, a common plant of the European and North American mountains, the proportion of the inflorescence given over to bulbil production (vivipary) increases with elevation, until in the most hostile environments there may be no seeds produced at all (**Plate 8.11**). Vivipary is an inherited character that is only triggered when the seed-bearing plants receive particular combinations of environmental factors associated with arctic or alpine environments. The most important trigger appears to be cold temperatures at the time of seed set.

Left: 8.11 *Polygonum viviparum* showing development of bulbils rather than seeds. Mangart, Slovenia, 2,100 metres.

Vegetative reproduction
Despite the evolutionary advantages of sexual reproduction, vegetative increase often predominates in arctic-alpine plants. This is because vegetative reproduction is less energy costly, and more likely to be successful in harsh arctic and alpine environments. Some species reproduce mainly by seed at lower elevations but predominantly by vegetative means at greater heights. Vegetative reproduction may involve highly developed special adaptations, as in vivipary and apomixis (see also Chapter 3) but is more commonly achieved by simple fragmentation of the 'parent' plant, and dispersal and establishment of the fragments.

A comment of Oleg Polunin's, following a trip to the Karakoram Mountains, is worth quoting here: 'I doubt whether much seed was set in the year of my visit. I concluded that the main methods of propagation and dispersal were by snow and earth movements, the crumbling of cliff sides, the flow of snow-melt water carrying pockets of soil containing living fragments of plants from one place to another' (Polunin, *The World of Rock Plants*, p. 96). It is important to appreciate this capability of many (and perhaps most) plant species, to produce new individuals from fragments when given reasonably favourable conditions. Even more common perhaps, in less violently disturbed environments, is the development of new individuals from fragments that remain attached to the parent plant until they are well rooted. By this means wide areas of ground may become colonized over time by a single clone. But connections between the ramets (individual pieces) of a clone may remain for long periods, and may exchange water and nutrients. In this case the whole collection of ramets may be regarded as functionally a single plant. This continuing interdependence probably helps clonal plants to withstand perturbations that would eliminate the individual ramets of which they are composed; this in turn enhances the resilience of plant communities that have a major long-lived clonal component.

Forms of Clonal Propagation

Eight main forms of clonal propagation have been identified in alpine plants:

1. Tussock graminoids (grasses, sedges and rushes), which form dense clusters of shoots with new ramets produced at one end while old ones die at the other.
2. Stoloniferous graminoids, either with below-ground stolons (horizontal stems), or producing widely spaced new ramets, able to colonize new open terrain or invade other vegetation (for example, *Luzula, Agrostis, Festuca*).
3. Mat-forming herbs that disintegrate at the middle as they spread outwards, rooting as they go at the tips (as in many *Phlox, Gentiana, Veronica*).
4. Stoloniferous or rhizomatous herbs, including snowbed plants such as many *Primula* and *Soldanella* and scree plants with long, often 'elastic' below-ground shoots that can grow rapidly and indefinitely when covered (as in many *Campanula* – see **Plate 8.12**, and *Linaria*).

Below: 8.12 *Campanula cochlearifolia* is a typical scree species which can withstand frequent burying and fragmentation. Dolomites.

5. Dwarf shrubs (many *Salix*, *Dryas* and *Pernettya*).
6. Viviparous plants that produce vegetative propagules (plantlets in *Poa alpina* ssp. *vivipara*, bulbils in *Polygonum viviparum*) in the flower heads.
7. 'Accidental' clonal plants that do not normally propagate clonally, but can do so on occasion when covered with a suitable rooting medium.

'Accidental' clonal plants include many species that may not be easy to propagate in cultivation by conventional cuttings, but can be increased by mounding them up with compost during their periods of active growth. Most ericaceous shrubs (including *Rhodothamnus chamaecistus*, cassiopes and dwarf rhododendrons) respond to this treatment, as do many cushion herbs (for example, *Dianthus*, some *Phlox*, *Draba* and *Androsace*). It is important that the cushion and compost are dry when the compost is applied, so that it may be easily worked down among the rosettes. The best time to do it is in spring, when flowering has ended and the plant is beginning to produce new growth; don't be too hasty in separating and potting the rooted pieces.

Life Expectancy of Alpine Plants

In the case of clonal reproduction the concept of individual ramet age becomes an irrelevance, since the clone may go on living almost indefinitely. DNA analysis of clonal ramets in *Carex curvula* suggests that individual clones may be several thousand years old; older in fact than the oldest Bristlecone pines. It is likely that the same applies to some dwarf willows, such as *Salix arctica*, and to ericoid shrubs, which can go on rooting at the margins indefinitely. Individual plants may also grow to a great age. It is estimated, for example, that large cushions of New Zealand 'vegetable sheep' (*Raoulia eximia*, *Haastia pulvinaris*), some up to several metres across, are many centuries old; this seems likely given that a cushion of *R. eximea* growing in a pot in the author's alpine house took ten years to grow to a diameter of 15 cm (6 in)! Similar, if less extreme, longevity is not unusual in alpines, particularly cushion plants, dwarf shrubs and tap-rooted perennials, such as pulsatillas and the larger meadow gentians. Fifty years would probably be a quite normal life span for such plants. Not only do many alpines have long individual life spans, but shorter-lived species often live longer than usual at higher elevations. Thus species that are annuals or biennials at low elevations may take three, five or even ten years to flower at high elevations.

9·FACTORS INFLUENCING THE ORIGINS AND PRESENT DISTRIBUTIONS OF ARCTIC AND ALPINE PLANTS

One of the most interesting aspects of the ecology of alpine plants, which can only be touched on here because of the complexity of the factors involved, concerns the origin of the species and the factors influencing their present distributions. The question of origins is particularly fraught with difficulties because of our hazy knowledge of the history of the Earth and the continents, and of past climates.

Origin of species
New species arise through natural selection acting upon individuals with particular combinations of genes. This is a continuous process and is the reason why there is variability within all species. However, when a group of individuals emerges all of which are sufficiently similar to each other, and sufficiently different from all others in a range of characteristics, we can say that a new species has arisen. The most important characteristic of a species is that, under normal conditions in the field, its members will not be able to cross-breed successfully with individuals of any other species. This does not mean that it can never happen in nature, or that inter-specific (or even inter-generic) hybrids cannot be induced artificially (we know that this is in fact a common occurrence in agriculture and horticulture), but it is the exception rather than the rule.

It is essential when thinking about evolution to try to think in terms of geological time, where millennia are analogous to seconds in a person's life (see Chapter 6). When viewing our present mountains and their plants we should do so in the same way that we look at a snapshot of some moment in our own lives. The living things in the photograph, including ourselves, are as they are because of the evolutionary processes that have formed them, over aeons of time. Just as we are the products of our ancestors back through the ages, and just as those ancestors originated from species quite different from ourselves, and living in different places, so the present-day alpines evolved from other plants, some of them alpines, some not, often at a great distance in space and time.

The rate of evolution varies in time and place, dependent to a great extent on the fitness of the species to the environment. This is influenced by a number of factors: firstly, the constancy or otherwise of that environment – species are able to persist for longer if their environment remains relatively unchanged; secondly, the genetic variability to be exploited within the species or, where the population is geographically or reproductively isolated, within the particular population of that species. Large variability in key genes within a population means that individuals with traits required for survival can be selected. Thus in any one mountain range at any given time some species are likely to be relatively stable (having evolved long ago to suit the prevailing environmental conditions that have remained relatively unchanged in recent times), while others will be undergoing rapid evolutionary change.

Endemic species

An endemic species is only found in a particular geographical area, which in the case of alpine plants may be a particular mountain, a group of mountains or a particular part of a geographical region or continent. Thus all the species in the genus Soldanella are endemic to the mountains of Europe, while the genus Dodecatheon, also in the Primulaceae, is restricted (endemic) to North America. Endemic genera or species have often been isolated from closely related plants for long periods of time, and may or may not have evolved further during such isolation. So endemic species from widely separated regions that have been isolated from each other for millennia may bear few resemblances to each other (as examples, the rosulate violas of the Andes compared to the 'typical' violas of the Northern Hemisphere), or may show striking similarities (as in the primulas of the Farinosae section from the extreme south of South America, compared to those of the Northern Hemisphere).

The best evidence for the evolution of new genera and species in mountain environments is the high proportion of endemic species in their floras. Endemic species are those which are only found in a particular geographical area. Certain genera and species are widely distributed and turn up in many mountain ranges,

often far apart. But most major mountain chains, especially if isolated from others (**Plate 9.1**), evolve species and, if sufficiently isolated, genera of their own. The genus Soldanella provides a good example of the latter, being currently restricted to the mountains of southern and eastern Europe, although it probably arose in the Quarternary period (from some 1.8 million years ago to the present), from an Asian ancestor similar to *Omphalogramma* (Zhang *et al.* 2001). At some stage an 'originator' Soldanella species (probably similar to S. *villosa*) became isolated from its ancestor, probably during a glacial period, and evolved quite quickly into a range of distinct, specialized, but very similar species, all being eventually restricted to alpine or montane habitats. It is likely that many other endemic alpines have evolved by natural selection in a similar way from ordinary populations of lowland plants (Love and Love 1974). The words 'likely' and 'probably' are used advisedly here because this is largely supposition. The fossil intermediates that would support such a case are lacking, indeed the representation of alpines within the fossil record generally is scant. This is because soil and climatic conditions in mountains do not favour the preservation of plant remains, unlike, for instance, those found in shallow lakes and lagoons. A possible source of information on the evolutionary development of alpine floras might be the preserved pollen and/or seeds that have remained buried in deep montane lakes and sediments, but there has been little investigation of this.

The new endemic species arising in mountains are often reproductively, as well as geographically, isolated and must survive or perish with the genes they have. Over past aeons of time many species, indeed whole genera and families of plants,

Above: 9.1 Isolated mountain ranges, such as the Pyrenees, tend to have a high proportion of endemic species. Vallé d'Aspe, Pyrenees.

will have perished. But as already noted, fossil evidence to prove this is lacking; nobody will ever know how many alpine species have evolved, and then subsequently succumbed when overwhelmed by changing environmental conditions.

Following on from this consideration of endemic plants it seems logical to postulate (and turns out to be true) that the number of species shared between mountain chains depends principally on their proximity. Isolated mountain ranges that develop rapidly, due to uplift, and near to older mountains (as in the Himalayas) gain species from them. The same is true when mountains develop near continuing and reliable sources of suitable plants such as the Arctic. As a result, endemics may form a rather low proportion of their floras. New mountains that are isolated from others by distance, or by habitats that are inhospitable to alpine plants (as is generally the case in the tropics), will tend to develop a higher proportion of endemic genera and species. The distances involved for the species to be isolated enough to develop measurable variability can be surprisingly small. Thus in a study of *Erysimum*, Sven Snogerup found that while populations growing on cliffs less than 500 metres (1,600 feet) apart were generally indistinguishable, those growing further apart than this were sometimes morphologically distinct (Rolfe, personal communication).

Plant geographers agree that the original arctic flora of perhaps 1,500 species must have reached a largely circumpolar distribution prior to the growth of the Greenland ice sheet (**Plate 9.2**) about 3 million years ago, which heralded the onset of the last Ice Age. As the climate deteriorated, and the ice sheet and glaciers

Above: 9.2 The Greenland ice sheet seen from 13,700 metres (45,000 ft). The 'nunataks' sticking up through the ice are the tops of mountains up to 4,900 m (16,000 ft) high. This photograph gives an impression of what much of any mountainous area affected by the ice would have looked like in the middle of a glacial episode.

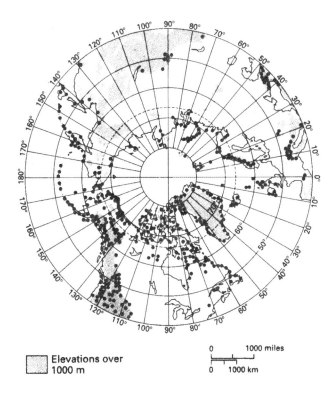

Elevations over
1000 m

0   1000 miles

0   1000 km

developed in the Arctic, the areas occupied by most of the formerly circumpolar plants were so radically split that they never recovered. This is evident from today's disjunct distribution of numerous species (**Figure 9.1**). When the glaciations began, the tundra was pressed southward but was also isolated in pockets surrounded by the ice further north. Some of the plant species that had become adapted to the mild arctic conditions of the Early Pliocene (3.5-5.3 million years ago) may not have kept the genetic plasticity needed for a relatively fast dispersal away from the increasing cold and the shortening of the growing season. So these succcumbed to natural selection without leaving a trace. Other species succeeded in escaping the glaciers. Some dispersed south into the lowlands or mountains of the normally temperate zone, which became considerably cooler during the glaciations. Others occupied islands and coast lands that were surrounded, but not overrun, by the ice. A few very hardy species were probably able to survive on ice-free nunataks (exposed hills or mountains) surrounded by the inland ice (Love and Love 1974).

The southern refugia (see Glossary) of the northern hemisphere were considerable in size. This was especially true near the coasts of eastern and western North America, in central Alaska, central Europe and eastern Siberia. These refugia were open southward for dispersal and allowed the movement of some northern species far south into the present lowlands of the temperate zone. Refugia were probably absent, or at least very restricted, south of the ice in the middle of the continents. This was because the glaciers prevented water runoff northwards, and caused the formation of enormous lakes to the south that drowned the vegetation before it could succumb to the cold (Love 1959).

Some of the arctic-alpines that are found today in mountains far to the south of their original Arctic 'strongholds' may have had very complicated histories. American alpine populations may be the result of southward dispersal during the glaciations, but the populations in central and southern Asiatic mountains are more likely to be *in situ* relics from the period before the glaciations, and are probably the ancestors of the arctic and American populations. This is probably true of various species such as *Vaccinium gaultherioides*, *Dryas octopetala*, *Diapensia lapponica* and some other arctic plants that have isolated occurrences on mountains in the temperate zone.

During the last two million years there have been some 20 cycles during which ice sheets have grown during cold (glacial) periods, and then retreated during intervening warmer (interglacial) episodes. It is often assumed that when the climate improved during the inter-glacials (including the current one, and after the most recent glaciation), the arctic-alpines that then occupied many lowland areas retreated northward with the ice and found refuges in temperate mountains. From what we know today, it appears that the plants that survived in the Arctic refugia (including those on nunataks) were more important in recolonizing the northern tundra than those moving northwards with the glaciers. Strong evidence supporting this hypothesis is provided by studies of variability in arctic and alpine races of a range of arctic-alpines in North America and Europe. These have shown that the different geographical races are genetically quite distinct (Crawford 1989). If there had been major plant immigration to the Arctic from the south over so short a period as the 10,000 or less years since the ice last retreated, we would expect plants in these two regions to be similar. That they are not suggests that the alpine populations of arctic-alpine plants that we grow have, in many cases, been isolated in their mountain strongholds for very long periods.

The Pleistocene glaciations were repeated several times. Each certainly caused the extinction of some species; it is likely that we now only have about half the species of arctic-alpines that were present before the glaciations began. Isolated populations of plants that survived the Ice Age's breaking up of the original circumpolar populations of the species sometimes evolved independently. This led in some cases to differentiation, and the development of plants with morphological differences that have warranted their recognition as species, subspecies or varieties. One example is the complex of arctic-alpine poppy species, which are similar but

nevertheless distinct. This group includes *Papaver relictum*, *P. radicatum*, *P. kluanense* and *P. alpinum* (**Plate 9.3**).

Some disjunct distributions of alpines are extraordinary, and difficult at first sight to explain. For example, primulas of the Farinosae group (*P. decipiens*, *P. magellanica* – see **Plate 9.4**) in the extreme south of South America and in the Falkland Islands, are separated by thousands of miles from their nearest relatives in North America. It used to be thought this indicated that primulas had formerly occurred throughout the Andes and that some climatic event(s) must have led to their extinction there – leaving only an isolated population. This is no longer believed to be the case, recent research having shown that other plants share this particular disjunct distribution between North and South America. In fact the flora of Tierra del Fuego in toto resembles that of the temperate mountains of North America more closely than it does any part of the Andes (Simpson and Todzia 1990). It has been suggested that this is because of the relative similarity of their present climates. In geological terms, the Falkland Islands and the Tierra del Fuego area emerged from ice cover very recently. So it appears likely that most if not all the species currently found in these regions are recent immigrants. Simpson and Todzia regard migrating birds as mainly responsible for the dispersal of many species to southern South America, since they would be arriving primarily from the mountains of western North America. Any one bird migrating from North to South America may have an infinitesimally small chance of successfully distributing the seed of a particular plant species. But if many birds do the trip, over

Above left: 9.3 *Papaver alpinum* ssp. *kerneri* is one of a group of similar but distinct alpine poppies found throughout the mountains of central Europe. Dolomites.

Above right: 9.4 *Primula magellanica*, photographed here in Petro Moreno National park, Argentina, is very similar in appearance to other members of the Farinosae group in North America, from which it is separated by thousands of miles of mountainous terrain containing no primulas.

millennia, there are almost certain to be occasional successes. These are all that are needed to set the colonization process – and evolution of new species – in motion.

There are many other equally fascinating, and mostly unexplained, disjunct distributions. Some have arisen as a result of continental drift (see Chapter 6). We now know that continents have moved, and often considerable distances, throughout geological time. They have not held fixed positions on the Earth's surface, or even always existed as individual, separate entities. **Figure 9.2** shows the most widely accepted history of these movements, starting from approximately 200 million years ago – when the continents were joined to form one supercontinent (Pangaea) – until the present time. By 135 million years ago, Pangaea had been divided into two continents by the formation of new ocean crust. These were Laurasia (today's North America, Europe and Asia) and Gondwanaland (South America, Africa, Antarctica, India and Australia) (**map B**). This was roughly the time when the first flowering plants began to appear on Earth. By 65 million years ago, when flowering plants were already well established, and evolving and spreading rapidly, Laurasia and Gondwanaland had fragmented into the continental masses we broadly recognize today (**map C**). However, North America and Eurasia remained connected, across what is now the North Atlantic, and North and South America remained separated, the Isthmus of Panama not forming until much later. Antarctica and Australia were also still connected, or just separating at this time.

While there is no evidence in the fossil record of alpines from this period, we do have good fossil evidence to support these continental movements. For example, Southern beeches (*Nothofagus* spp.) currently occur in the south of South America, and in Australasia, and in the fossil record of Antarctica. It is unlikely that Nothofagus seeds could survive long distance transport by ocean currents, and much more feasible that they once occurred throughout the southern part of Gondwanaland. Similarly, cycads are currently widely distributed throughout tropical and sub-tropical regions of the world. This might seem strange, since they have large rounded seeds of the type typically dispersed over short distances through their ability to roll, and are not dispersed by ocean currents because they sink in water. With seeds that are too large, heavy and dense to be carried great distances by birds, wind or ocean currents, it appears mysterious that they have such a wide

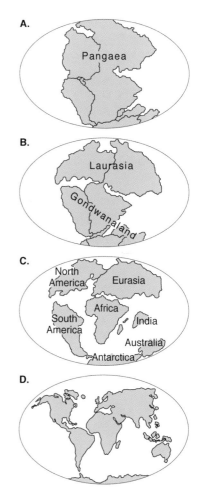

Figure 9.2
Possible history of continental drift since the Earth was formed.

distribution. But it would be quite possible if the continents they are found in were once united.

So perhaps some of our modern alpines have ancient ancestors (in some cases very similar to them, in others very different) that colonized whole continents that were once united but are now separate. Unfortunately we shall never know for sure. In the meantime we may imagine that this was perhaps the case where *Rhodothamnus chamaecistus* (**Plate 9.5**) and *Kalmiopsis leachiana* are concerned. The two species can be easily confused on casual inspection and are sufficiently compatible, genetically, to be hybridized in cultivation. But *Rhodothamnus* occurs only in the European mountains, while *Kalmiopsis* occurs only in the Columbia River Gorge of western North America. Did they share a common ancestor that once grew throughout Eurasia, and across the then North Atlantic land bridge? Was there a Eurasian link across what is now the Bering Sea? If so, how long ago was the ancestral link, how did it break, and why? These and many similar questions may never be answered, but there are those of us who will get much pleasure from trying.

Left: 9.5 *Rhodothamnus chamaecistus*, seen here in the Julian Alps, occurs only in the central European mountains but has a look-alike cousin (*Kalmiopsis leachiana*) which occurs only in Oregon, 8,000 miles away.

10·IMPACTS OF GLOBAL CLIMATE CHANGE ON ALPINE PLANTS

The climate of the earth has always been volatile, changing from hour to hour, day to day, season to season and year to year; nowhere more so than in the mountains, as we have seen in Chapter 4. All organisms have to be able to cope with these routine short-term temporal changes in climate. But there have also been quite separate, overall longer-term trends of underlying climate change. During the last 2-3 million years there have been a number of glaciations alternating with warmer interglacial periods, some of which have been considerably warmer than the one we are living in today. These colder and warmer periods have generally alternated on a time scale of thousands of years, or longer. But there is increasing evidence from the geological record (including ice cores, which can provide clues to past climate) that suggests there have been abrupt changes in temperature at the end of a cold or warm period, perhaps within a few tens or hundreds of years. The reasons for these so-called 'flips' – from cold to warm climate and *vice-versa* – are currently the subject of intense debate and intensive research. This is because we need to know whether current global warming is due primarily to natural processes (a 'flip'), as some scientists believe; to man's activities; or through a combination of both. Global warming has been closely tracked by warming in the mountains of the Northern Hemisphere (**Figure 10.1**) that is itself unprecedented in recent centuries. Whatever the reasons, major climate changes are underway throughout the world, as indicated by both the marked retreat of the glaciers in all the major mountain chains of the Northern Hemisphere, and the fragmentation of parts of the Antarctic ice sheet.

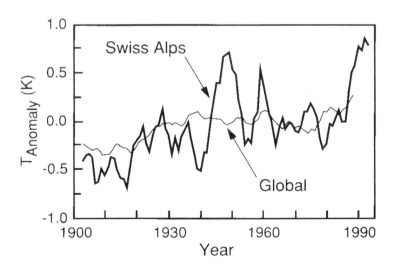

Figure 10.1
A comparison of mean surface temperature warming (°K [°C]) at eight high elevation sites in the Swiss Alps during the 20th century with global trends over the same period.
(Beniston *et al.* 1997)

The meaning of global climate change
The climate of the Earth is constantly changing with the seasons, from day to day and hour to hour. On a larger scale, some years, or even decades, are warmer or colder, wetter or drier than average. Living organisms, including alpine plants, have to be able to survive these normal climatic vicissitudes. But what we are witnessing now is a prolonged, steady – but, in Earth systems terms, rapid – warming of the Earth's atmosphere, at a rate that is unprecedented in recent millennia. Glaciers and ice fields are retreating rapidly throughout the mountains and higher latitudes of the Northern Hemisphere. Present projections indicate that there will be little permanent ice and snow on European mountains by the end of the 21st century. Such warming brings an associated loss of snow cover. Both are likely to have dramatic effects on the distribution and abundance of particular types of alpine habitat (sub-alpine woodland, alpine meadow, snowbeds, tundra and rock ledges); this will greatly affect the species that inhabit them. Some sensitive species are likely to become extinct, either locally or throughout their ranges.

Though as yet unproved, it is probable that current global warming is substantially increased by man's activities, notably the production of 'greenhouse gases' (carbon dioxide, or CO_2) from the burning of fossil fuels. If so, it will only be reversed by the widespread adoption of technologies and lifestyles that reduce their use. But carbon dioxide remains in the atmosphere for a long time. So, by the time such reductions are widely adopted and take effect, it may well be too late for many alpine species.

The interacting factors in the Earth system that control climate are extremely complex and difficult to model, even with the most sophisticated computer techniques and processing power available. This makes it difficult to assess what climate changes may be occurring. While predictions of future climate are improving all the time, they are currently still too simplistic to do more than indicate general trends. Those who would like to learn more about this fascinating subject are referred to E G Nisbet's very readable text, *Leaving Eden: To protect and Manage the Earth* (Nisbet 1991).

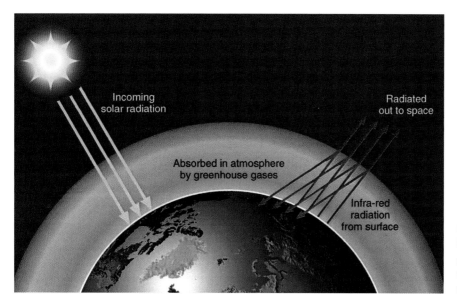

Figure 10.2
Diagram of how the
greenhouse effect operates
to enhance surface
temperatures on Earth.

The argument regarding man's influence on global climate change hinges on the importance of the so-called 'greenhouse effect'. We know that concentrations of some 'greenhouse gases', notably carbon dioxide (CO_2), have increased continually, and more or less exponentially, since the start of the industrial revolution. This is as a result of burning fossil fuels. These gases accumulate in the upper atmosphere and act in a way similar to the glass in a greenhouse. Incoming solar radiation readily passes through gases such as CO_2, in the same way it does through the glass in a greenhouse. But radiant (infrared) heat from the Earth's surface is partially absorbed by the gas and this warms the lower atmosphere (**Figure 10.2**). Most predictions for climate change suggest that warming will accelerate during this century unless there is a major and sustained reduction in worldwide CO_2 emissions. It is believed that warming will be greatest at high latitudes, especially in the Arctic (for a review of the likely impacts there, see Kullman 1994), and there is evidence already to support this: recent studies show that the sub-arctic tree line is extending northwards, in places as far apart as the Canadian north and Siberia (see Chapter 4 for an account of the significance of tree lines in alpine ecology). It would be expected that the maximum limit for vegetation is also advancing northwards in places. But it is less easy to get clear evidence of this because the sparse arctic-alpine plant cover, unlike trees, is not detectable on air photographs and satellite images. However, the potential for arctic-alpines to migrate northwards is thought to be good. Populations of most species (for example, *Dryas octopetala* and *Silene acaulis*) are large and dispersed over a wide latitudinal range, with land bridges linking different populations. And there is plenty of potentially suitable land for plants to colonize.

Assured success is less likely for plants migrating upwards in mountains. But, nevertheless, there is widespread evidence that alpine species have migrated upwards during the warming trend of the past few decades (see Walther *et al.* 2002 for a recent review). Recently, a careful re-survey of the limits of vegetation in Alpine areas that were surveyed decades earlier (Grabherr and Pauli 1994) confirmed trends already suggested by Braun-Blanquet (1956). They had noted increased plant species' presence above 3,000 metres (9,850 feet) elevation in 1947-55, compared with 1812-35. More recently, Klanderund and Birks (cited in Birks 2003) have carried out a similar re-survey in the Jotunheimen mountains of Norway. They surveyed over 400 localities on 24 mountains that had been surveyed by Jorgensen in 1930-1. A wide range of sub-alpine shrubs and grasses had expanded their upper altitudinal limits over the 66-year interval by an average of 200-300 metres (660-980 feet). Over the same period high alpines had decreased in abundance. Birks suggests that this may be due to a combination of the direct effects of climate warming and the indirect effects of increased competition from the faster-growing species that were expanding from lower elevations.

A particular problem with climate change is likely to develop in mountains where plant migration upwards is curtailed by limited elevational range. To survive, plants migrating upwards above the existing limit of vegetation must be able to find a suitable alpine habitat that is currently plant-free. If there is none, there is nowhere for them to go. In Europe, the Pyrenees, Carpathians and Apennines come immediately to mind, but there are many other mountain ranges throughout the world with little potential for upward migration of alpine floras. It also needs to be appreciated that montane floras generally include some small, isolated endemic populations that are often very specialized. Even in the higher mountains, some of the species involved may be unable to migrate fast enough to avoid being overcome by more aggressive competing species, also migrating upwards in response to the milder climate. Thus there is the distinct possibility that some species will be forced into local, and perhaps total, extinction, while other more competitive species are favoured by the change. Those species most at risk are likely to live only within narrow thermal (effectively, altitudinal) ranges (Holten 1993; Saetersdal and Birks 1997). They will probably be slow growing, with short-range seed dispersal (few, large seeds and no aids for wind or animal dispersal). Most of the rarer high alpine, rock crevice specialists fall into this category. Many have evolved relatively large seeds (for the size of the plant) that are ideally suited for passive dispersal into suitable adjacent rock crevices because this is where they have the best chance of survival. This is fine at present, but not when rapidly changing climate demands faster, longer-range dispersal for survival.

Research into how plants might respond to climate change has been done in the high Arctic, Alaska and the Alps. Artificial warming of tundra vegetation suggests that, in general, there will be little or no increase in overall growth at higher temperatures. Instead, plant phenology (the annual cycle of growth and development) will be accelerated. The lack of a significant growth response suggests that productivity in tundra is constrained by the indirect effects of cold temperatures (such as low nutrient availability or short growing season length) rather than by cold growing-season temperatures themselves (Hobbie and Chapin, 1998). But there do appear to be big differences in response to warming between species. For example, *Dryas octopetala* (**Plate 10.1**) growing in the Arctic generally responded positively to warming by growing more and setting more seed (Wookey *et al.* 1995). On the other hand, *Cassiope tetragona* (Havstrom *et al.* 1993) and *Saxifraga oppositifolia* (**Plate 10.2**) (Stenström *et al.* 1997) were much less responsive. In the case of *Cassiope tetragona* there were substantial differences in response to temperature between populations; those from the highest latitudes or altitudes responded most. These responses to increased temperature were shown to be affected by the relative importance of temperature as a limiting factor for growth and development in these environments compared with other limiting factors (nutrients, light). The relative importance of these different factors is in turn influenced by latitude, elevation and soils. Nevertheless, it was clear from these studies that some species are inherently more 'plastic' in their responses to a whole range of environmental factors. Where plants are in competition, these plants are likely to win out, at the expense of the others.

Below left: 10.1 In field experiments *Dryas octopetala* responded positively to warmer temperatures.

Below right: 10.2 However, the growth of *Saxifraga oppositifolia* decreased as temperatures rose.

In addition to its indirect effect via air temperature change, there is growing evidence that increases in atmospheric CO_2 may directly affect the survival and growth of plants growing in the wild. Elevated CO_2 has been used for many years in commercial glasshouses as a way to increase crop production. It does this by acting as a source of carbon for photosynthesis. But under controlled glasshouse conditions all other potentially limiting factors (light, water, nutrients) can be supplied in abundance. It was thought that, in nature, shortage of one or other of these other essential components for photosynthesis might often limit a plant's potential to respond to increased CO_2 – so protecting it. While this may often be so, evidence from montane studies suggests that CO_2 does have direct effects. As in the case of elevated temperature, different (even closely related) species vary in their responses. In a recent study in the Jura Mountains, in Switzerland (Fischer *et al.* 1997), a gentian (G. *cruciata* – **Plate 10.3**) and a gentianella (G. *germanica* – **Plate 10.4**) were transplanted into species-rich grassland plots. These were subsequently exposed to elevated levels of CO_2. Growth and survival of the gentian was unaffected, whereas the gentianella suffered, survival being reduced by half (compared with controls at ambient CO_2). The difference was due to the

Above left: 10.3 *Gentiana cruciata* responded positively to elevated levels of atmospheric carbon dioxide.

Above right: 10.4 In contrast, growth of *Gentianella germanica* was reduced by half.

ability of G. *cruciata* to respond positively to the extra carbon dioxide, whereas G. *germanica* was unable to respond. G. *cruciata* grew more vigorously, and in doing so held its own against responsive competing species. However, this study also showed that there was a large genetic variation in response to CO_2 between seedlots of G. *germanica*. This suggested that some populations would have a better chance of survival than others as CO_2 levels increase.

Another possible effect of increasing CO_2 on alpines might be reduced frost tolerance. Studies on a range of plants (though, unfortunately, none of them were alpines) have shown marked increases in damage at temperatures near to freezing, under controlled conditions of CO_2 and temperature. Alpines that are inherently frost sensitive, such as snowbed species, might be particularly prone to damage. There are likely to be an almost infinite number of similar, often very subtle interactions between species in response to increasing CO_2. This makes it very difficult to predict exactly what the effects on particular species might be in particular situations.

As far as the alpine gardener is concerned, the principal effect of climate change is likely to be increased difficulty in cultivating alpines at low elevations due to climate warming. Many of the problems in growing high alpines in temperate environments result from the lack of a reliable cold spell in winter; alternating freeze and thaw are anathema to plants that are adapted to a long winter rest. This problem can only increase if winters become warmer. It will be difficult for the cultivator to keep his or her plants cold enough to prevent them coming into growth early, at a time when their resistance to pests and diseases is at a minimum. Perhaps chilling beds in winter will become commonplace, like those used in the alpine house at Kew, that allow the rooting zone to be kept at a constant cold temperature.

It is possible that quite the opposite of climate warming might occur in northern Europe, along the western Atlantic seaboard. This region currently benefits from its proximity to the Gulf Stream's warming effect. The warm, salty waters of the Gulf cool as it flows northwards, and become more saline in the process. Salt water is heavier than fresh water, and around Iceland, and between Labrador and Greenland, the water sinks beneath less salty water. It then flows southwards again, but at deeper oceanic levels, and is known as the North Atlantic Deepwater Current. Continued melting of the Arctic ice, due to global warming, is pouring millions of tons of fresh water into the North Atlantic. The fear is that, if this continues, the salinity of the water at the places in the Nordic seas where the Gulf Stream currently sinks may be greatly reduced. This may lead to a cessation of the Gulf Stream-North Atlantic Deepwater Current 'conveyor'. If this happened, the climate of maritime north-west Europe would become much like that at similar latitudes on the eastern seaboard of the USA, with pack ice in winter and broken-up sea ice in summer.

In areas where summer heat already makes the cultivation of high alpines difficult, a further increase in summer temperatures due to global warming is likely to make things even worse. Shading, to reduce insolation, may be a possibility in some areas but not in others, especially those where humidity is as much of a problem as heat. Perhaps the large electric fan I once saw being used *outdoors* to keep alpines cool in a hot and sticky New York garden was not such an eccentric idea after all!

Changed patterns of rainfall are another major aspect of climate change, likely to affect the cultivation of alpine plants. For example, trends indicate that British gardens will endure even wetter winters than normal, increasing the need for cultivation techniques that ensure perfect drainage. Sand beds and crevice gardens are likely to become more popular among those who strive to grow the more difficult high alpines in the open garden. Others may resort to the use of more cover, but find that this only exacerbates the accompanying problems from increasingly warmer winters.

Climate change is sure to further test the ingenuity and skill of alpine gardeners. But, after all, overcoming challenges has always been a central characteristic of the true alpine grower.

GLOSSARY

A horizon: the layer of a soil profile lying immediately below the litter layer (if present) and above the subsoil or '**B horizon**'.

Aestivation: passing the summer in a dry or dormant condition.

Anoxia: lack or absence of oxygen.

Apical meristems, *see* **meristems**

Apomixis: asexual reproduction, including the formation of seeds without sexual reproduction, and vegetative reproduction.

Asexual reproduction: not involving the fusion of male and female **gametes.**

Asthenosphere: (from an invented Greek *a* + *sthenos* 'without strength') is the region of the Earth between 100-200 km (62-124 miles) below the surface – but perhaps extending as deep as 400 km (248 miles) – that is the weak or 'soft' zone in the upper mantle. It lies just below the **lithosphere**, which is involved in plate movements and **isostatic** adjustments.

B horizon: the layer of a soil profile lying below the **A horizon** and above the mineral substratum (C horizon).

Biosphere: the part of the Earth's surface and atmosphere inhabited by living things.

Bryophytes: mosses and liverworts.

Bulbil: small bulb that develops above ground from a bud. Bulbils may form on the stem from axillary buds.

Calcifuge plant: a plant that does not tolerate alkaline (basic) soil. The word is derived from the Latin 'to flee from chalk'.

Carbon accumulation: net gain of carbon by a plant when **photosynthesis** exceeds **respiration**.

Cell organelle: a structural and functional unit within a cell, such as a nucleus, mitochondrion or chloroplast.

Cell sap: the fluid medium within the cell within which the cell organelles are borne.

Chemical germination inhibitors: natural chemicals within seeds that inhibit germination.

Chilling bed: structure for providing constant cold temperatures to simulate montane environments for alpine plants in cultivation.

Chlorosis: a yellowing of leaf tissue, usually especially marked between the veins, due to a lack of chlorophyll.

Circumpolar distribution: (of plants) in which a plant species occurs very widely in suitable habitats around the northern or southern polar regions.

Cloche: a loose term that describes any structure used to protect plants in the open ground from adverse environmental conditions.

Clone: a number of **ramets** that belong to the same **genet**.

Cold hardening: the physiological process whereby plants become gradually inured to damage by cold or frost through the progressive reduction of the temperature to which they are exposed.

Columnar: having the form or shape of a column.

Compromise strategies: strategies evolved by plants for survival, growth or reproduction that involve balances between different, sometimes conflicting, options.

Concentration gradient: the graduated difference in concentration of a solute per unit distance through a solution.

Continental drift: the theory that the Earth's continents move gradually over the surface of the planet on a substratum of magma. The present-day configuration of the continents is thought to be the result of fragmentation of a single landmass, Pangaea, that existed some 200 million years ago.

Convergent evolution: the evolutionary development of a superficial resemblance between unrelated organisms that occupy a similar environment.

Crevice garden: garden (or trough) rockwork which attempts to mimic natural outcrops primarily occurring in sedimentary or metamorphic rock with planar cleavage, providing crevices with many different aspects and slopes suited to a wide range of alpine plants.

Cross-pollination: the transfer of pollen from the anthers of one flower to the stigma(s) of another flower by insects, wind etc.

Crustose plants: bryophytes or lichens that form a crust over rocks, vegetation etc.

Cultivar: contraction of the words 'cultivated' and 'variety'. A plant raised or selected in cultivation that retains distinct, uniform characteristics when propagated by appropriate methods.

Cuticle: the protective layer that protects the outer cells (epidermis) of higher plants.

Cyanobacteria: (Greek: *kuavos* 'blue') a phylum (or 'division') of bacteria that obtain their energy through **photosynthesis**. They are often referred to as blue-green algae. The description is primarily used to reflect their appearance and ecological role rather than their evolutionary lineage.

Dicotyledon: any flowering plant of the Class *Dicotyledonae*, having two embryonic seed leaves and net-veined leaves (cf. **monocotyledon**).

Diffusion gradient: a gradient in concentration of atoms or molecules diffusing within a liquid or gas.

Disjunct distribution: when the occurrence of a plant species is discontinuous despite the apparent availability of suitable habitat in the intervening terrain.

Diurnal temperature fluctuations: changes in temperature over a 24-hour period, normally associated with night and day.

Early successional species: plants

that typically colonise areas of bare or recently disturbed ground (cf. **late successional species**).

Ecosystem: a system involving interactions between a community of living organisms and its non-living components.

Ecotype: a group of organisms within a species that occurs in a particular habitat or place and that differs from other groups within the same species occurring in different habitats or locations.

Edaphic: (Greek: *edaphos* 'ground, soil') 1. Of or relating to soil, especially as it affects living organisms. 2. Influenced by the soil rather than by the climate.

Endemic species: found only in a particular geographical area or region.

Endemism: the process of evolving **endemic species**.

Entomophilous: pollinated by insects.

Ericoid shrubs: woody plants in the family Ericaceae.

Etiolated: drawn up and/or yellowed as a result of restricted access to light.

Facultative apomixis: partial or incomplete **apomixis**.

Fellfield: the zone of steep, often shattered rock, and permanent snow and ice above the alpine meadows, home to some of the choicest high alpines and often characterised by a particularly rich **bryophyte** and **lichen** flora.

Fitness (of a species): suitability of a species to its habitat developed through evolutionary processes.

Fossil record: the occurrence of fossils giving evidence of past occurrence and distribution of particular species of organisms.

Freeze-thaw: the alternating cycle of above- and below-zero (centigrade) temperatures leading to physical weathering of rocks and movements of rocks and soil.

Frost heave: the upthrust and cracking of a ground surface through the freezing and consequent expansion of water in or below it.

Frost hummocks: formed in soils at high altitudes or latitudes due to action of **frost-heaving**. The overall result is a pattern of alternating mounds and depressions over the land.

Frost tolerance: the ability of a plant to withstand freezing temperatures without death or serious damage.

Gamete: a reproductive cell.

Gene: a unit of heredity, capable of replication and mutation, occupying a fixed position on a chromosome and transmitted from parent to offspring during reproduction.

Genet: a genetic individual, resulting from a single sexual fusion, consisting of one to many **ramets**, and usually genetically distinct from all other genets.

Genetic variability: variability between individuals with respect to their genes.

Geographical races: populations of organisms occurring in particular geographical locations that are distinct from those occurring in other places.

Germination inhibitor: substance present in the seed that inhibits its ability to germinate under otherwise suitable conditions.

Germination requirements: the factors required for a seed to germinate, normally including oxygen, water and a suitable temperature regime.

Global warming: increase in global temperature, especially that believed to be due to anthropogenic causes.

Gondwanaland: a hypothetical southern continental mass of the late Palaeozoic and Mesozoic eras that included Antarctica, South America, Africa, India, and Australasia (cf. **Laurasia**).

Greenhouse effect: warming of the Earth's atmosphere due to the presence of substances (notably carbon dioxide) in the upper atmosphere that inhibit the escape of heat, much as the glass does in a greenhouse.

Greenhouse gases: those gases (principally carbon dioxide, methane and oxides of nitrogen) that when present in the upper atmosphere inhibit the escape of heat from the Earth's surface.

Gulf Stream: a relatively warm ocean current flowing north-eastwards off the Atlantic coast of North America, from the Gulf of Mexico.

Habitat niche: location/opportunity within a habitat suitable for occupation by particular species.

Heliotropism: the growth of a plant in response to the stimulus of sunlight

Herbivory: feeding by animals on plants.

Higher plants: plants with a vascular system for transport of water and other materials, including ferns, conifers and flowering plants.

Humic acids: soluble soil acids derived from the decomposition of organic remains.

Hybridization: crossing of genetically unlike individuals.

Hydrophytic: an environment having abundant supplies of water.

Ice cores: core samples from the accumulation of snow and ice over many years that have recrystallized and have trapped air bubbles from previous time periods. The composition of these ice cores, especially in the presence of hydrogen and oxygen isotopes, provides a picture of the climate at the time.

Inflorescence: a branch, or system of branches, bearing two or more individual flowers.

Insect pollinator preferences: the preference of pollinating insects for the flowers of particular kinds of flowers (form, colour, scent etc.) or particular species.

Insolation: the incoming solar radiation that reaches a planet and its atmosphere or, by extension, any object exposed to solar rays, such as a plant.

Interglacial episodes: periods of relative warming that occur between colder periods of glacial expansion (ice ages).

Invasion: plant colonization of a particular habitat niche.

Irradiation: the process by which an item is exposed to radiation. The exposure can be intentional, sometimes to serve a specific purpose, or it can be accidental. In common usage the term refers specifically to ionizing radiation, and to a level of radiation that will serve that specific purpose, rather than radiation exposure to normal levels of background radiation or abnormal levels of radiation due to accidental exposure.

Isolated population: population of plants that is effectively separated from other populations of the same species.

Isostacy/Isostatic: a term used in geology to refer to the state of gravitational equilibrium between the Earth's **lithosphere** and **asthenosphere** such that the **tectonic plates** 'float' at an elevation which depends on their thickness and density. It is invoked to explain how different topographic heights can exist at the Earth's surface.

Krummholz: dwarfed trees at or near the treeline in montane and polar regions.

Land bridge: continuous, often relatively narrow piece of land that provides(ed) a bridge between larger areas of land.

Landslip: the sliding of a large mass of rock, soil, etc., down the side of a mountain or cliff, or the material dislodged in this way.

Late successional species: species that normally arrive in a habitat only when it already has significant vegetation cover (cf. **early successional species**).

Latitudinal gradient in biodiversity: a gradient in species' abundance associated with a particular change in latitude.

Laurasia: hypothetical mass of land in the northern hemisphere in the Palaezoic era that later separated to form the northern continents (cf. **Gondwanaland**).

Leaf dry mass: weight of a leaf when dried to constant mass.

Lichen: a lower 'plant' which is formed by the symbiotic association of a fungus and an alga.

Lithosphere: the solid outermost shell of a rocky planet. On the Earth, the lithosphere includes the crust and the uppermost layer of the mantle (the upper mantle or lower lithosphere) which is joined to the crust.

Lower plant: simple nonvascular plant, including green algae and **bryophytes.**

Macroclimate: the climate affecting a geographical region or locality (cf. **microclimate**).

Macro-environment: the environment in the general vicinity in which a plant grows (cf. **micro-environment**).

Maturation: the process of maturing or ripening.

Meltwater: the water resulting from the seasonal melting of snow and ice.

Meristem: (including **apical meristem**) a tissue inplant consisting of undifferentiated cells (meristematic cells) found in zones of the plant where growth can take place – the roots and shoots. Apical occur at the tips of shoots or roots and are responsible for increasing their length.

Mesophytic: an environment having a moderate amount of water.

Microbial pathogen: a disease-causing microscopic organism.

Microclimate: the climate in the immediate vicinity of a plant, e.g. at the leaf surface, which is often influenced by the plant itself and its neighbours (cf. **macroclimate**).

Macro-element: an element required by plants in substantial amounts for their healthy growth (cf. **micro-element**).

Micro-element: an element required by plants only in trace amounts for their healthy growth (cf. **macro-element**).

Micro-environment: the environment surrounding a plant and often influenced by it and its neighbours (cf. **macro-environment**).

Microflora: a community of microscopic plants (including fungi), especially in the soil or on the surfaces of plants.

Micro-organism: any sub-microscopic organism, but generally used particularly to denote fungi and bacteria.

Micro-topography: small variations in ground form that may affect **micro-climate** and **micro-environment**.

Mollusc: an animal of the order *Mollusca*, which in horticulture refers to slugs and snails.

Monocotyledon: any plant of the Class *Monocotyledonae*, having a single embryonic seed leaf and (generally) parallel-veined leaves (cf. **dicotyledon**).

Mosaic: an intricate mixture of different plant species or vegetation types.

Mycorrhizas: the result of symbiotic (mutually beneficial) associations between fungi and plant roots. This symbiotic association provides the fungus with a renewable source of food through access to fixed carbon (sugars) from plant photosynthate. In return, the plant gains the use of the mycelium's tremendous surface area to absorb mineral nutrients from the soil.

Natural selection: a process resulting

in the survival of those individuals from a population of plants or animals that are best fitted to the prevailing environmental conditions. The survivors tend to produce more offspring than those less well fitted, so changing the composition of the population and the gene combinations that are available for further selection.

Net photosynthesis: the net amount of carbon fixed, allowing for that lost by respiration.

Niche: *see* **habitat niche**.

Non-graminaceous: not a member of the grass family (*Gramineae*).

Nunatak: an area of land that is surrounded by ice but not covered by it, with special reference to glaciation.

Nutrient cycling: the processes in the Earth's atmosphere, water bodies and (especially) soils by which nutrients become available to plants.

Ovule: a small body in the ovary of a seed-bearing plant that contains the egg cell which develops into the seed after fertilization.

Pangaea: an ancient landmass that is thought to have split up at the end of the Palaeozoic era into the continents of **Gondwanaland** and **Laurasia**.

Paramo, cushion: high-elevation, treeless ecosystem in the Andes, characterized by a predominance of cushion plants.

Permafrost: ground that is permanently frozen, often to great depths, the surface sometimes thawing in summer.

Phenology: the study of recurring phenomena, in the case of plants, usually seasonal patterns of growth and development.

Photosynthesis: the synthesis of energy-rich carbohydrates from carbon dioxide and water using sunlight captured by chlorophyll in the chloroplasts of green plants.

Photosynthetic capacity: the effectiveness of a plant in carrying out **photosynthesis**.

Phyto-microclimate: a microclimate formed in the immediate vicinity of a plant due to the presence and/or physiological activity of the plant itself.

Photosynthetic carbon gain: the net fixation of carbon by **photosynthesis**.

Plant adaptation: the ability of a plant species or individual to survive, grow and reproduce under a particular set of environmental conditions.

Plant biomass: amount of plant material, normally referring to living material only but may be broadened to include persistent dead remains.

Plant breeding systems: the mechanisms by which plants ensure successful reproduction.

Plant immigration: the colonization of a habitat or geographical space by plants from outside that habitat or space.

Plant migration: the movement of plants from one geographical region to another, particularly (for the purposes of this book) under the influence of changing climate.

Pollination: the transfer of pollen from the anthers to the stigma.

Propagule: any structure having the capacity to give rise to a new plant, whether through sexual or asexual (vegetative) reproduction.

Radiation stress: stress experienced by plants exposed to high levels of solar radiation, particularly plants emerging from snow cover.

Ramet: a physiologically independent individual, one to many of which may make up a **genet** (genetically distinct population of individuals) or **clone**.

Refugium(a): a geographical region that has remained unaltered by a climate change event affecting surrounding regions, and that therefore forms a haven for relict flora and fauna.

Resilient ecosystems: ecosystems that maintain or regain their diagnostic characteristics following disturbance.

Respiration: the chemical breakdown of complex organic substances, such as carbohydrates and fats, that takes place in the tissues of plants and animals, during which energy is released and carbon dioxide produced.

Rhizomatous: a plant having a **rhizome** or rhizomes**.**

Rhizome: a thick, horizontal underground stem that is both a food storage organ and, when fragmented, a means of reproduction.

Root:shoot ratio: the proportion of roots to shoots, usually measured by a comparison of the dry weights of above- and below-ground parts of plants. Alpine plants often have unusually high root:shoot ratios.

Sand beds: beds composed entirely of coarse sand for growing plants from arid regions in gardens with wet climates.

Scarification: physical or chemical abrasion of hard-coated seeds to aid germination.

Seed bank: the repository of seeds lying dormant in the soil that may germinate given suitable conditions.

Seed dispersal strategies: the various means evolved by plants to aid the dispersal of seeds, including such aids as wings and 'parachutes' for wind dispersal, and attractive fruits and hooks for animal dispersal.

Seed predation: consumption of seeds by animals.

Seed set: commencement of seed development following successful fertilization.

Seed-coat inhibition: inhibition of seed germination caused by the presence of impermeable or impenetrable seed coats and/or the presence therein of chemical germination inhibitors.

Seedlot: individual collection of seed from a distinct group of plants.

Selection pressures: factors acting on living organisms that influence the progress of **natural selection**.

Sexual reproduction: the union of a male **gamete** in the pollen grain with a female gamete in the ovule to produce a viable seed.

Snow gliding: the dispersal of seed on the surface of compacted snow and ice.

Snow mould: a fungus that attacks plants while they lie dormant beneath snow cover.

Snowbed: an area of ground which, because of its topography, receives deep snow cover each winter.

Snowbed vegetation: vegetation that is covered by snow for a prolonged period in winter, including specialist species that are not found elsewhere.

Snowmelt: water produced in spring by the melting of snow and ice.

Soil acidification: the process whereby soil becomes gradually more acid. This occurs naturally, particularly in soils derived from acidic or neutral rocks, because rainwater is slightly acidic, but may be accelerated by the presence of acidic industrial pollutants dissolved from the atmosphere.

Soil creep: the gradual movement of soil downslope due to repeated freeze-thaw cycles.

Soil-forming materials: weathered rock fragments, disturbed subsoil etc. that have the potential to form soils.

Soil polygons: areas of soil with similar characteristics delimited by polygon shapes for soil mapping purposes.

Soil stripes: regular linear patterns caused by various agencies such as **soil creep**, **solifluction**, wind and water erosion.

Solifluction: slow downhill movement of soil, saturated with meltwater, over a permanently frozen subsoil in tundra regions.

Species richness: abundance of different species in a particular plant community or locality.

Stoloniferous graminoids: grasses and their allies that spread and may reproduce vegetatively by means of **stolons**.

Stoloniferous herbs: herbaceous flowering plants, other than grasses, that spread and may reproduce by means of **stolons**.

Stolons: shoots that bend to the ground or that grow horizontally above the ground and produce roots and shoots at the nodes.

Sub-arborescent: having a woody base but no permanent tree-like woody structure.

Succession: more or less ordered pattern of change in the species composition of vegetation through time at a particular location, generally associated with increasing stability.

Sun tracking: continued positive orientation of plant parts, particularly flowers, towards the sun as it tracks across the sky (**heliotropism**).

Supercontinent: landmass which existed in geological time that split up to form two or more of the current continents.

Super-cooling: cooling of a liquid without freezing or crystallization to a temperature below that at which freezing or crystallization should occur.

Surfactant: a wetting agent.

Tectonic plates: the **lithosphere** essentially 'floats' on the **asthenosphere**. The lithosphere is broken up into what are called tectonic plates – in the case of Earth, there are ten major and many minor plates. These plates move in relation to one another. Earthquakes, volcanic activity, mountain-building, and oceanic trench formation occur along plate boundaries.

Thermal insulation: insulation of a plant or its parts from cold temperature extremes, e.g. by the presence of hairs or spines that slow down wind movement.

Tree line: the upper limit of natural tree growth (elevational or latitudinal) that forms the boundary between sub-alpine (sub-arctic) and alpine (arctic) zones.

Tuber: a swollen underground stem (e.g. potato) or root (e.g. dahlia) that is an organ of vegetative reproduction and food storage.

Tundra: treeless zone lying between the timber line and the zone of permanent snow and ice, having permanently frozen subsoil.

Tussock graminoids: grasses and their allies that have a characteristic tussocky form.

Upward migration: movement of alpine vegetation uphill in response to climate warming.

Vegetative (clonal) reproduction: reproduction that does not involve seed production but perpetuates the **clone.**

Viviparous plant: one that either produces seeds that germinate before separating from the parent plant, or bulbils or young plants instead of flowers.

Vivipary *see* **viviparous plant**.

Waxy cuticle: the outer waxy surface layer of the leaf.

Xerophytic: an environment having very little available water.

Zonation of vegetation: occurrence of different plant communities in zones, often related to environmental factors such as climate or soil type.

REFERENCES

Books and book chapters

Brooks, R R (1987). *Serpentine and its Vegetation: a Multidisciplinary Approach*. Portland, OR: Dioscorides Press.

Billings, W D. 'Arctic and alpine vegetation: plant adaptations to cold summer climates'. 403-444 in ed. Ives, J D, Barry, R G and Alford D K (1974). *Arctic and Alpine Environments*. London: Methuen.

Beck, E. 'Cold tolerance in tropical alpine plants'. 77-110 in ed. Rundell, P W, Smith A P and Meinzer, F C (1994). *Tropical Alpine Environments*. Cambridge: Cambridge University Press.

Cherrett, J M. 'Key concepts: the results of a survey of our members' opinions': 1-16 in ed. J M Cherrett (1990). *Ecological Concepts: The contribution of Ecology to an Understanding of the Natural World (Symposium of the British Ecological Society)*. Oxford: Blackwell Scientific Publications.

Crawford, R M M (1989). *Studies in Plant Survival: Ecological Case Histories of Plant Adaptation to Adversity*. Oxford: Blackwell Scientific Publications.

Crawley, M J (1983). *Herbivory: the Dynamics of Animal-plant Interactions*. Berkeley: University of California Press.

Deno, N C (1993) (and supplements, 1996 and 1998). *Seed Germination Theory and Practice* (2nd Edition). Available only from Professor Norman C Deno, 123 Lenoir Drive, State College, PA 16801, USA.

Deshmukh, I (1986). *Ecology and Tropical Biology*. Oxford: Blackwell Scientific Publications.

Ellis, P R, Entwistle, A R and Walkey, D G A (1993). *Pests and Diseases of Alpine Plants*. Alpine Garden Society, Pershore, England.

Fitter, A H. 'Nutrient acquisition'. 51-72 in ed. Crawley, M J (1997). *Plant Ecology* (2nd edition). Oxford: Blackwell Scientific Publications.

Geiger, R (1965). *The Climate Near the Ground*. Cambridge, MA: Harvard University Press.

Goldstein, G, Meinzer, F C and Rada, F. 'Environmental biology of a tropical treeline species, *Polylepis sericea*. 129-149 in ed. Rundell P W, Smith, A P and Meinzer, F C (1994). *Tropical Alpine Environments*. Cambridge: Cambridge University Press.

Holten, J I. 'Potential effects of climatic change on distribution of plant species, with emphasis on Norway'. 84-104 in ed Holten J I, Paulsen G and Oechel, W C (1993). *Impacts of Climatic Change on Natural Ecosystems, with Emphasis on Boreal and Arctic alpine areas*. Trondheim: NINA.

Körner, C (1999). *Alpine Plant Life*. Berlin: Springer-Verlag.

Kruckeberg, A R (1984). *California serpentines: Flora, vegetation, geology, soils and management problems*. Berkeley: University of California Press.

Kruckeberg, A R. 'Plant life of western North American ultramafics'. 31-73 in ed. Roberts, B A and Proctor, J (1993). *The Ecology of Areas with Serpentinized rocks*. Dordrecht, Netherlands: Kluwer Academic Publishers.

Love, A and Love, D. 'Origin and evolution of the arctic and alpine floras'. 571-603 in ed. Ives, D J and Barry, R G (1974). *Arctic and Alpine Environments*. London: Methuen.

Lyons, K G. 'An introduction to the serpentine plant community of the Putah-Cache watershed'. 257-259 in ed. Boyer A J, Goggans J, Leroy D, Robertson D and Thayer R (2001). *Putah and Cache: a Thinking Mammal's Guide to the watershed*. Davis, CA: University of California at Davis Press.

Marrs, R H, Roberts, R D, Skeffington, R A and Bradshaw, A D. 'Nitrogen and the development of ecosystems'. 113-136 in ed. Lee, J A, McNeill S and Roirison, I A (1981). *Nitrogen as an Ecological Factor*. Oxford: Blackwell Scientific Publications.

McAleese, A J, Rankin, D W H and Sun Hang (1999). 'Rhododendrons do grow on limestone'. *The New Plantsman* 6: 23-29.

McAleese, A J and Rankin, D W H (2000). 'Growing rhododendrons on limestone soils: Is it really possible?' *Journal of the American Rhododendron Society* 54: 126-134.

Nisbet, E G (1991). *Leaving Eden: To Protect and Manage the Earth*. Cambridge: Cambridge University Press.

Pisek, A, Larcher, W and Unterholsner, R (1967). *Kardinale Temperaturbereiche der Photosynthese und Grenztemperaturen des Lebens der Blätter verscheidener Spermatophyten. I Temperaturminimum der der Nettoassimilation, Gefrier und Frostschadensbereiche der Blätter*. Flora Abt. B, 157: 239-264.

Polunin, O. 'Himalayan Alpines from the Karakoram to Nepal'. 94-106 in ed. Elliott, R C (1971). *The World of Rock Plants (A report of the 4th International Rock Garden Plant*

Conference 1971). London: Alpine Garden Society.

Ram, J, Singh, S P and Singh, J S (1988). 'Community level phenology of grassland above treeline in Central Himalaya, India'. *Arctic and Alpine Research* 20: 325-332.

Rankin, D W H. 'Rhododendrons on limestone, wild and in cultivation'. 31-44 in *Alpines 2001, Conference Report* (2001). Pershore (England): Alpine Garden Society.

ed. Sakai, A and Larcher, W (1987). *Frost Survival of Plants. Responses and Adaptation to Freezing Stress. Ecological Studies: Analysis and Synthesis*, vol. 62, Berlin: Springer-Verlag.

Smith, A P. 'Introduction to tropical alpine vegetation'. 1-19 in ed. Rundel, P W, Smith A P and Meinzer, F C (1994). *Tropical Alpine Environments*. Cambridge: Cambridge University Press.

Tranquillini, W (1979). *Physiological Ecology of the Timberline*. New York: Springer-Verlag.

Vitousek, P M and Walker, L R. 'Colonization, succession and resource availability: Ecosystem-level interactions'. 207-223 in ed. Gray, A J, Crawley, M J and Edwards, P J (1987). *Colonization, Succession and Stability, 26th Symposium of the British Ecological Society*. Oxford: Blackwell Scientific Publications.

Periodical articles

Atken, O K, Botman, B and Lambers, H (1996). 'The causes of inherently slow growth in alpine plants: an analysis based on the underlying carbon economies of alpine and lowland Poa species'. *Functional Ecology* 10: 698-707.

Aydelotte, A R and Diggle P.K

(1997). 'Analysis of developmental preformation in the alpine herb, *Caltha leptosepala*'. *American Journal of Botany* 84: 1648-1657.

Beniston, M, Diaz, H E and Bradley, R S (1997). 'Climate change at high elevation sites: An overview'. *Climate Change* 36: 233-251.

Bilbrough, C J, Welker, J M and Bowman, W D (2000). 'Early spring nitrogen uptake by snow-covered plants: a comparison of Arctic and alpine plant function under the snowpack'. *Arctic and Alpine Research* 32: 404-411.

Billings, W D and Mooney, H A (1968). 'The ecology of arctic and alpine plants'. *Biological Review* 43: 481-529.

Birks, J H B (2003). 'Alpines and extremes'. *The Alpine Gardener: Bulletin of the Alpine Garden Society* 71: 86-98.

Bliss, L C (1971). 'Arctic and alpine plant life cycles'. *Annual Review of Ecology and Systematics* 2: 405-438.

Blundon, D J and Dale, M R T (1990). 'Dinitrogen fixation (acetylene reduction) in primary succession near Mount Robson, British Columbia, Canada'. *Arctic and Alpine Research* 22: 255-263.

Bowman, W D (1992). 'Inputs and storage of nitrogen in winter snowpack in an alpine ecosystem'. *Arctic and Alpine Research* 24: 211-215.

Bowman, W D and Steltzer, H (1998). 'Positive feedbacks to anthropogenic nitrogen deposition in Rocky Mountain Alpine Tundra'. *Ambio* 27: 514-517.

Bowman, W D, Schardt, J C and Schmidt, S K (1996). 'Symbiotic N_2-fixation in alpine tundra: ecosystem input and variation in fixation rates

among communities'. *Oecologia* 108: 345-350.

Braun-Blanquet, J (1956). 'Ein Jahrhundert Florenwandel am Piz Linard (3414 m)'. *Bulletin Jardin Botanique Bruxelles* 26: 221-232.

Caldwell, M M (1968). 'Solar ultraviolet radiation as an ecological factor for alpine plants'. *Ecological Monographs* 38: 243-268.

Caldwell, M M, Robberecht, R and Billings, W D (1980). 'A steep latitudinal gradient of solar ultraviolet-B radiation in the arctic-alpine life zone'. *Ecology* 61: 600-611.

Chambers, J C, McMahon, J A and Brown, R W (1990). 'Alpine seedling establishment: the influence of disturbance type'. *Ecology* 71: 1323-1341.

Diggle, P K (1997). 'Extreme preformation in alpine *Polygonum viviparum*: an architectural and developmental analysis'. *American Journal of Botany* 84: 154-169.

Eckel, O and Thams, C (1939). 'Untersuchungen über Dichte, Temperatur und Strahlungsverhältnisse der Schneedecke von Davos'. *Beiträge zur Geologie der Schweiz: Hydrologie* 3: 275-340.

Fahey, B D (1974). 'Seasonal frost heave and frost penetration measurements in the Indian Peaks region of the Colorado Front Range'. *Arctic and Alpine Research* 6: 63-70.

Fischer, H and Kuhn, H W (1984). 'Diurnal courses of temperatures in cushion plants'. *Flora Jena* 175: 117-134.

Fischer, M, Matthies, D and Schmid, B (1997). 'Responses of rare calcareous grassland plants to elevated CO_2 : a field experiment with *Gentianella germanica* and *Gentiana cruciata*'. *Journal of Ecology* 85: 681-691.

Galen, C (1990). 'Limits to the distribution of alpine tundra plants: herbivores and the alpine skypilot'. *Polemonium viscosum. Oikos* 59: 355-358.

Galen, C and Stanton, M L (1995). 'Responses of snowbed plant species to changes in growing-season length'. *Ecology* 76: 1546-57.

Gardes, M and Dahlberg, A (1996). 'Mycorrhizal diversity in arctic and alpine tundra: an open question'. *New Phytologist* 133: 147-157.

Geber, M A (1985). 'The relationship of plant size to self-pollination'. *Mertensia ciliata. Ecology* 66: 762-772.

Gibson, N and Kirkpatrick, J B (1985). 'Vegetation and flora associated with localized snow accumulation at Mount Field West, Tasmania'. *Australian Journal of Ecology* 10: 91-99.

Godley, E J (1979). 'Research in the vegetation of New Zealand'. *New Zealand Journal of Botany* 17: 441-446.

Gómez, J M, Zamora, R, Hódar, J and Garcia, D (1996). 'Experimental study of pollination by ants in Mediterranean high mountain and arid habitats'. *Oecologia* 105: 236-242.

Good, J E G (1974-1975). 'Rock garden plants from seeds'(six parts, in two volumes). *Quarterly Bulletin of the Alpine Garden Society* 42: 135-142, 239-242, 319-334 and 43: 69-71, 153-167, 246-258.

Grabherr, G and Pauli, M G H (1994). 'Climate effects on mountain plants'. *Nature* 369: 448.

Halliwell, B (1981). 'A new alpine house at Kew'. *Quarterly Bulletin of the Alpine Garden Society* 49: 23-25.

Hamerlynck, E P and Smith,W K (1994). 'Subnivean and emergent microclimate, photosynthesis, and growth in *Erythronium grandiflorum* Pursh, a snowbank geophyte'. *Arctic and Alpine Research* 26: 21-28.

Harder, L D and Barrett, S C H (1995). 'Mating cost of large floral displays in hermaphrodite plants'. *Nature* 373: 512-515.

Havstrom, M, Callaghan, T V and Jonasson, S (1993). 'Differential growth responses of *Cassiope tetragona*, an arctic dwarf-shrub, to environmental perturbations among three contrasting high- and subarctic sites'. *Oikos* 66: 389-402.

Heinrich, B (1979). 'Resource heterogeneity and pattersn of movement in foraging bumblebees'. *Oecologia* 40: 235-245.

Hobbie, S E and Chapin, F S (1998). 'Response of tundra plant biomass, aboveground production, nitrogen, and CO_2 flux to experimental warming'. *Ecology* 79: 1526-1544.

Holmen, K (1957). 'The vascular plants of Pearey Land, North Greenland'. *Meddr Gronland* 124: 1-149.

Humphries, H C, Coffin, D P and Lauenroth, W K (1996). 'An individual-based model of alpine plant distributions'. *Ecological Modelling* 84: 99-126.

Johnson P L and Billings, W D (1962). 'The alpine vegetation of the Beartooth Plateau in relation to cryopedogenic processes and patterns'. *Ecological Monographs* 32: 105-135.

Jordan, D N and Smith W K (1995). 'Microclimate factors influencing the frequency and duration of growth season frost for subalpine plants'.

Agricultural and Forest Meteorology 77: 17-30.

Junnila, S (1985). 'Seasonal changes in cold hardiness of *Diapensia lapponica*'. *Proceedings of the 4th Oikos Conference on Winter Ecology*, Oulu, Finland, September 12-13, 1984, 81-85.

Kevan, P G (1990). 'Sexual differences in temperatures of blossoms on a dioecious plant, *Salix arctica*: significance for life in the Arctic'. *Arctic and Alpine Research* 22: 283-289.

Krog, J (1955). 'Notes on temperature and N_2 gas measurements indicative of special organization in arctic and subarctic plants for utilization of radiated heat from the sun'. *Physiologia Plantarum* 8: 836-839.

Kudo, G (1991). 'Effects of snow-free period on the phenology of alpine plants inhabiting snow patches'. *Arctic and Alpine Research* 23: 436-433.

Kudo, G (1992). 'Performance and phenology of alpine herbs along a snow-melting gradient'. *Ecological Research* 7: 297-304.

Kudo, G and Suzuki, S (2002). 'Relationships between flowering phenology and fruit-set of dwarf shrubs in alpine fellfields in northern Japan: a comparison with a subarctic heathland in northern Sweden'. *Arctic and Alpine Research* 34: 185-190.

Kullman, L (1994). 'Climate and environmental change at high northern latitudes'. *Progress in Physical Geography* 18: 124-135.

Larcher, W (1980). 'Klimastress im Gebirge – Adaptationstraining und Selektionsfilter für Pflanzen'. *Rheinisch Westfäl Akad. Wiss. (Düsseldorf) Naturwiss. Vortr* 291: 49-88.

Larigauderie, A and Körner, C (1995). 'Acclimation of leaf dark respiration to temperature in alpine and lowland plant species'. *Annals of Botany* 76: 245-252.

Lawler, D M (1988). 'Environmental limits of needle ice: a global survey'. *Arctic and Alpine Research* 20: 137-159.

Love, D (1959). 'The postglacial development of the flora of Manitoba: a discussion'. *Canadian Journal of Botany* 37: 547-585.

Luzar, N and Gottsberger, G (2001). 'Flower heliotropism and floral heating of five alpine plant species and the effect on flower visiting in *Ranunculus montanus* in the Austrian Alps'. *Arctic and Alpine Research* 33: 93-99.

Mark, A F (1965). 'Flowering, seeding and seedling establishment of narrow-leaved snow tussock, *Chionochloa rigida*'. *New Zealand Journal of Botany* 3: 180-193.

Mark, A F (1994). 'Patterned ground activity in a southern New Zealand high-alpine cushionfield'. *Arctic and Alpine Research* 26: 270-280.

Mark, A F and Adams N M (1979). *New Zealand Alpine Plants*. (2nd edition). Christchurch, NZ: A H & A W Reed Ltd.

McGraw, J B (1985). 'Experimental ecology of *Dryas octopetala* ecotypes: relative response to competition'. *New Phytologist* 100: 233-241.

Michalet, R, Gandoy, C, Joud, D, Pagès,J and Choler, P (2002). 'Plant community composition and biomass on calcareous and siliceous substrates in the northern French Alps: comparative effects of soil chemistry and water status'. *Arctic and Alpine Research* 34: 102-113.

Molau, U (1993). 'Relationships between flowering phenology and life history strategies in tundra plants'. *Arctic and Alpine Research* 25: 391-402.

Montalvo, A M (1994). 'Inbreeding depression and maternal effects in *Aquilegia caerulea*, a partially selfing plant'. *Ecology* 75: 2395-2409.

Moser, W, Brzoska, W, Zachuber, K and Larcher, W (1977). 'Ergebnisse des IBP-Projekts "Hoher Nebelkogel 3184 m"'. Sitzungsber. Oesterrd. Akad. Wiss. (Wien) Math. Naturwiss. Kl Abt. I/186: 387-419.

Mullen, R B, Schmidt, S K and Jaeger, C H (1998). 'Nitrogen uptake during snowmelt by the Snow buttercup'. *Ranunculus adoneus. Arctic and Alpine Research* 30:121-125.

Munn, L C, Buchanan, B A and Nielsen, G A (1978). 'Soil temperatures in adjacent high elevation forests and meadows of Montana'. *Soil Society of America Journal* 42: 982-983.

Muñoz, A A and Arroyo, M T K (2002). 'Postdispersal seed predation on *Sisyrinchium arenarium* (Iridaceae) at two elevations in the central Chilean Andes'. *Arctic and Alpine Research* 34: 178-184.

Ohara, M and Higashi, S (1994). 'Effects of inflorescence size on visits from pollinators and seed set of *Corydalis ambigua* (Papaveraceae)'. *Oecologia* 98: 25-30.

Ramsey, M (1995). 'Ant pollination of the perennial herb *Blandfordia grandiflora* (Liliaceae)'. *Oikos* 74: 265-272.

Richards, A J (1995). 'White flowers and the New Zealand flora'. *Quarterly Bulletin of the Alpine Garden Society* 63: 275-278.

Saetersdal, M and Birks, H J B (1997). 'A comparative ecological study of Norwegian mountain plants in relation to possible future climatic change'. *Journal of Biogeography* 24: 127-152.

Schaefer, J A and Messier, F (1995). 'Scale-dependent correlations of Arctic vegetation and snow cover'. *Arctic and Alpine Research* 27: 38-43.

Scherff, E J, Galen, C and Stanton, M L (1994). 'Seed dispersal, seedling survival and habitat affinity in a snowbed plant: limits to the distribution of the snow buttercup, *Ranunculus adoneus*'. *Oikos* 69: 405-413.

Schlag, R N and Erschbamer, B (2000). 'Germination and establishment of seedlings on a glacier foreland in the central Alps, Austria'. *Arctic and Alpine Research* 32: 270-277.

Seastedt, T R and Vaccaro, L (2001). 'Plant species richness, productivity, and nitrogen and phosphorus limitation across a snowpack gradient in alpine tundra, Colorado, U.S.A'. *Arctic and Alpine Research* 33: 100-06.

Shibata, O and Nishida, T (1993). 'Seasonal changes in sugar and starch content of the alpine snowbed plants, *Primula cuneifolia* ssp. *hakusanensis* and *Fauria crista-galli*, in Japan'. *Arctic and Alpine Research* 25: 207-210.

Simpson, B B and Todzia, C A (1990). 'Patterns and processes in the development of the high Andean flora'. *American Journal of Botany* 77: 1419-1432.

Spira, T P and Pollak, O D (1986). 'Comparative reproductive biology of alpine biennial and perennial gentians (*Gentiana*: Gentianaceae) in California'. *American Journal of Botany* 73: 39-47.

References

Stanton, M L, Rekmanek, M and Galen, C (1994). 'Changes in vegetation and soil fertility along a predictable snowmelt gradient in the Mosquito Range, Colorado, USA'. *Arctic and Alpine Research* 26: 364-374.

Stenström, M, Gugerli, F and Henry, G H R (1997). 'Response of *Saxifraga oppositifolia* L. to simulated climate change at three contrasting latitudes'. *Global Change Biology* 3/Supplement 1, 44-54.

Stöcklin, J and Bäumler, E (1996). 'Seed rain, seedling establishment and clonal growth strategies on a glacier foreland'. *Journal of Vegetation Science* 7: 45-56.

Sullivan, J H, Teramura, A H and Ziska, L H (1992). 'Variation in UV-B sensitivity in plants from a 3,000-m elevational gradient in Hawaii'. *American Journal of Botany* 79: 737-743.

Theodose, T A, Jaeger, C H III, Bowman, W D and Schardt, J C (1996). 'Uptake and allocation of ^{15}N in alpine plants: implications for the importance of competitive ability in predicting community structure in a stressful environment'. *Oikos* 75: 59-66.

Tod, H (1971). 'Chlorosis in rhododendrons'. *Gardener's Chronicle and Horticultural Trades Journal* 170: 17-25.

Tyler, G (1994). 'A new approach to understanding the calcifuge habit of plants'. *Annals of Botany* 73: 327-330.

Wade, L and McVean, D (1969). Mt. *Wilhelm Studies I. The Alpine and Subalpine Vegetation*. Canberra: Australian National University, Research School of Pacific Studies Publication BG/1.

Walther, G-R, Post, E, Convey, P, Menzel, A, Parmesan, C, Beebee, T J C, Fromentin, J-M, Hoegh-Guldberg, O and Bairlein, F (2002). 'Ecological responses to recent climate change'. *Nature* 416: 389-395.

Wookey, P A, Robinson, C H, Parsons, A N, Welker, J M, Press, M C, Callaghan, T C and Lee, J A (1995). 'Environmental constraints on the growth, photosynthesis and reproductive development of *Dryas octopetala* at a high Arctic polar semi-desert, Svalbard'. *Oecologia* 102: 478-489.

Zhang, L-B, Comes, H P and Kadereit, J W (2001). 'Phylogeny and quarternary history of the European montane/alpine endemic *Soldanella* (Primulaceae) based on ITS and AFLP variation'. *American Journal of Botany* 88: 2331-45.

Zimov, S A, Zimova, G M, Daviodov, S P, Daviodova, A I, Voropaev, Y V, Voropaeva, Z V, Prosiqnnikoh, S F, Prosiannikova, O V, Semilatova, I V and Semiletov, I P (1993). 'Winter biotic activity and production of CO_2 in Siberian soils: a factor in the greenhouse effect'. *Journal of Geophysics Research* 98: 5017-23.

INDEX